THE TR

WITHDRAWN

BBC MUSIC GUIDES

The Trio Sonata

CHRISTOPHER HOGWOOD

BRITISH BROADCASTING CORPORATION

For Jan Smaczny

Contents

Published by the
British Broadcasting Corporation
35 Marylebone High Street
London W1M 4AA

ISBN 0 563 17095 6

First published 1979

© Christopher Hogwood 1979

Typeset in Great Britain by Eta Services (Typesetters) Ltd., Beccles, Suffolk
Printed in England by Whitstable Litho Ltd., Whitstable, Kent

Introduction

In 1732 the Abbé Pluche was able to declare that 'Sonatas are to music what mottled paper is to painting' – adding, to clinch the matter, that 'sonatas are not much pleasure for the public'. His remarks were directed, naturally for a Frenchman, against the Italians, the nation which had evolved and dominated all the major musical forms of the baroque – sonata, cantata, concerto and opera. The public, however, thought otherwise: thanks to the enthusiasm of baroque composers, publishers and players, both amateur and professional, we now possess some eight thousand examples of the form that failed to convert the Abbé.

It is curious, though, that the trio sonata, the most popular example of the form and the one that was clearly the most profitable to produce, should nowadays be so neglected, while its classical counterpart – the essentially Germanic string quartet – flourishes as the epitome of the chamber music idiom.

This summary cannot hope to do more than establish some of the principles of thought that lay behind the trio sonata, the national characteristics that conditioned its development and the way this Italianate form was transmitted and eventually accepted throughout Europe. The territory, however, is so vast, and so much of it, at the moment, inaccessible, that any survey will amount to an aerial view, 'a *general Map*', to quote Pope, 'marking out no more than the *greater parts*, their *extent*, their *limits* and their *connection*'.[1]

---

[1] William S. Newman's study of *The Sonata in the Baroque Era* (3rd ed., New York, 1972) cannot escape immediate recommendation, however, as the most invaluable Baedeker any investigator could desire.

The Trio Sonata Concept

The first stumbling block in any approach to the trio sonata is its terminology. Almost no trio sonata was written for three performers. Titles such as *Sonate a tre*, *Sonnatas of Three Parts* and so on meant sonatas for which three part-books were needed; the bass part, often figured, would normally involve two players reading from the same book – a sustaining bass instrument, such as the cello or bass viol, and a chordal instrument, such as the harpsichord, organ or lute. A typical trio sonata group would therefore consist of two violins, cello and harpsichord. Trio sonatas *could,* however, require anything from a single player (Bach's organ trios, for example) to a complete orchestra (the *Orchestra Trios* of Johann Stamitz), while still fulfilling the condition of being written in three parts.

But not all writing in three parts was conceived according to the concept of the trio sonata. The range of techniques can be indicated by three samples (Ex. 1). The first is an example of the consort fantasia style, written on the verge of the trio-sonata era. Its three parts are of equal importance and together produce a harmonically self-contained structure without the support of a keyboard instrument. The second shows a polarisation of thought towards two equal soprano parts dependent on the bass part (abbreviated hereafter as SSB); in the third example the first violin part has all the melodic interest, while the second violin and continuo provide harmonic support. The first and third examples are unexceptional extracts from Thomas Tomkins and Sammartini respectively and represent the territory immediately outside the true trio sonata; but the second example is from the collection of trios by Corelli, which was the most influential single source of the whole period, and which forms a central reference point for all discussion of the trio sonata. Corelli's detractors, incidentally, took such exception to this particular passage that a ten-year controversy raged in Italy over its faults and merits (see page 41n. for details).

Chronology is a poor guide to the development of musical thought at the best of times, especially in a period so frontier-conscious as the baroque. So it is less valuable to track the trio sonata year by year from Tomkins to Sammartini than to isolate the virus where it first occurred and then plot the course of the infection through the body of Europe. In some areas the initial

Ex.1

(a)

(b)

(c) **Andante affettuoso**

Vln. 1

Vln. 2

B.C.

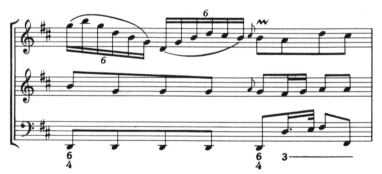

resistance was considerable and forceful (*vide* Abbé Pluche and others in France); other centres such as Vienna, well placed on the arteries of musical circulation, succumbed to the fever in its early days.

The basic carrier of the infection was an Italian product, the violin, whose growing dominance was assisted by the development of music publishing and printing in Venice. Northern Europe, exhausted by the efforts and deprivations of the Thirty Years War, and by continuing political troubles, was particularly susceptible to foreign influence. The trio sonata, with its polarisation of resources into two equal treble instruments and an independent melodic and harmonic bass, was an inexpensive means of maintaining musical performance, so integral a part of court life throughout Europe. It was also the perfect meeting ground for the rival claims of the old vocal music and the new instrumental styles, and could adapt the old ideas of polyphony to the new concept of accompanied melody. Many countries might have made the discovery; Italy was the first to announce that it had, with sonatas by Cima in 1610.

Italian terminology for the trio sonata reveals distinctions which have been ironed out by modern titling.[1] The title of *Sonata a due col basso* indicated variations in the treatment of the bass part between string bass and keyboard bass; that of *Sonata a tre* meant a more emphatic division of labour. In some cases the continuo bass provided a simplified version of the string bass part, while in the most extreme examples the string bass took a totally independent line and produced what amounts to a quartet texture. Compare, for example, part of a Purcell trio sonata, where the 'Thorough Bass' plays a simplified version of the figurations in the bass viol part, with Cavalli's scoring of the chaconne at the end of his *Canzona a 3* which (at this point only in the whole work) is effectively in four parts—Ex. 2 overleaf.

This distinction in terminology accounts for the apparent discrepancy between the two sets of trio sonatas by Purcell; the first, published during his lifetime, was described as *Sonnata's of III Parts*, while the second set was put out by his widow in 1697 as *Sonata's in Four Parts*. The scoring, however, is the same in both cases, with separate part-books for the bass viol and the continuo.

[1] For a full discussion of the Italian 'Solo, Duo and Trio Sonata', see N. M. Jensen in *Festskrift Jens Peter Larsen*, p. 73.

Ex.2

(a) Purcell (Sonata V, 1683)

(b) Cavalli

In his remarks 'To the Reader' before the 'three-part' sonatas, Purcell explained that the collection would have been published sooner 'but that he has now thought fit to cause the whole Thorough Bass to be Engraven, which was a thing quite besides his first Resolutions'.[1] Evidently his publisher was not prepared to re-engrave the title page as well. In fact, only one movement of the 1683 collection (the Largo of Sonata V) contains passages in true four-part writing.

Another variant of Italian titling was to describe the bass part as being for 'violone o cembalo', a designation followed by English publishers such as Walsh with *Twelve Sonatas for two Violins, with a bass for Violoncello or Harpsichord*. It is clear that in most cases this was merely a convenience of grammar, the title answering the question 'Whose music stand does the part belong to?' It made little difference when both players shared the same part – except to the comfort of the violoncellist craning his neck, as in many en-

[1] See p. 84 for Purcell's complete text.

gravings, to see the music over the harpsichordist's shoulder – and it was sufficiently arbitrary in some cases for the title page to say 'or' and the parts to say 'and': Vivaldi's Op. 1, for instance, or Valentini's Op. 4.[1] Occasionally, the choice was real, however. Sammartini offered trios 'a due violini, e violoncello, e cembalo, se piace, opera terza' in London *c*.1745, and as the century went on it seems that continuo-less performances became more frequent.

As so often in the development of the trio sonata, we are faced with evidence of the interrelationship between the notated music and contemporary performing practice; few other forms reflect the influence of improvisation on musical construction. The convention of the figured bass is the most obvious example of musical shorthand, but other techniques such as the simplification of the continuo bass line and the omission of a string bass were anticipated in performance instructions before the results were apparent in notated music. Nicolai Matteis (*False Consonances of Musick*) recommended the keyboard player to leave elaborate figuration to the bass viol and play only the harmonic outline, as was also indicated in Purcell's publications (see p. 87).

Occasionally we find modern performance assumptions upset by original indications. Corelli's trios, for instance, suggested the use of the archlute as an alternative not to the organ, but to the violoncello (see p. 41), although we would nowadays assume it to be a chord-playing instrument. Other authors adopted a casual attitude to the addition or subtraction of instruments which the twentieth century has not yet emulated; Bononcini suggests optional viola parts for trio sonatas, while Domenico Gabrieli (1684) and Bassani, in his Op. 1 of 1677, describe their second violin parts as 'ad libitum'.

Sometimes commercial interest intervened, for example in the sets of sonatas (frequent in the mid-eighteenth century) said to be for 'violins, oboes or flutes' but featuring double-stopping and going well beyond the range of the wind instruments. Similarly the Italian alternative of *violino o cornetto*, especially popular during the first thirty years of the seventeenth century, resulted from the fact that string players and wind players belonged to different guilds, each of which would feel obliged to buy the sonatas in question.

[1] Contrary to modern expectation, there is no source to be found in Italy before 1700 which specifies the obligatory addition of a string bass to the 'continuo' line (see N. M. Jensen, *op. cit.*).

Despite the flexibility revealed in titling, the standard grouping for the trio sonata in the eighteenth century was two violins, violoncello and keyboard. This preference was reflected in the largest extrapolation of the trio sonata concept into the *concerto grosso* form. Although modern analysis tends to work from the largest form down to the smallest, practicality as well as business sense encouraged the baroque composer to view things from the opposite direction; a *concerto grosso* was simply a trio sonata writ large, as many title pages advised their customers: *Concerti Grossi con duoi Violini, e Violoncello di Concertino obligati, e duoi altri Violini, Viola e Basso ad arbitrio che si potranno radoppiare.*[1] Not all *concerti grossi* could be played in their most reduced form – it was perhaps to make such chamber performances more complete that Pepusch included the viola in the *concertino* group when he made the first full-score of Corelli's *concerti grossi* in 1732. Georg Muffat (who knew both Corelli and Lully) described more variety for the performance of such works than is ever countenanced today, and appropriately, began with the essential trio:

You may form a perfect little trio, at all times necessary, from the following voices: Violino primo concertino, Violino secundo concertino, and Basso continuo e Violoncino concertino. Your bass, however, will go better on the small French bass than on the double bass used hereabouts, and to this may be added, for the greater ornamentation of the harmony, a harpsichord or theorbo, played from the very same part. Further, it is to be noted that, besides observing the directions *piano* and *forte*, all should play with a full tone at the direction *T* or *tutti*, softly and tenderly at the direction *S* or *solo*.[2]

Only after adding the two viola parts to the trio did Muffat suggest, as the next stage, the addition of the *ripieno* violins and basses. As a final alternative, he even suggested experimenting with wind players as a solo trio:

Should there be among your musicians some who can play and control the French oboe or shawm agreeably, you may with the best effect use two of these instead of the two violins, and a good bassoon player instead of the French bass, to form the concertino or little trio in some of these concertos.

Commercial initiative apart, however, the use of alternative scorings diminished throughout the seventeenth century. With the

[1] From Corelli's Op. 6: 'Concerti Grossi for two violins and violoncello as the essential solo group, plus parts for two other violins, viola and bass to taste, which may be doubled'.

[2] From *Auserlesene Instrumental-Musik,* 1701.

exception of regional preferences, such as the North German partiality for wind instruments, the violin family proved most adaptable in ensemble, and could accommodate the greatest variety of idiom and expression. This adaptability and expressive potential was summed up, with a certain hyperbole, by Giovanni Doni in 1640:

In the hand of a skilful player, the violin represents the sweetness of the lute, the suavity of the viol, the majesty of the harp, the force of the trumpet, the vivacity of the fife, the sadness of the flute, the pathetic quality of the cornett; as if every variety, as in the great edifice of the organ, is heard with marvellous artifice.[3]

The new idiom of the violin was naturally seen at its most flamboyant in solo sonatas and concertos, but it was equally influential, though less demonstrative, in controlling the development of the texture of the trio sonata. While the richness of the bass line lay in its own divisibility, with internal variety ranging from the simplest sequence of sustaining harmonies to the greatest independence of 'figurate' string writing with keyboard harmonies behind, the essence of trio-sonata thought was the unity of the upper parts. Merely to add a second violin part to an existing treble did not of itself create a trio sonata (see, for instance, Matteis or Geminiani). 'The work of a 3rd part' according to Roger North 'is not onely to fill the consort, but also to bear its part of the air . . . both [treble parts] have their turnes and alternately take the upper hand, as the master thinks fitt to compose them'. The added 'second treble' on the other hand 'comonly abates of the agillity affected in the other; but taken as it is used in the French musick, nothing can be more unpleasant and dull. . . .'[2] Purcell, discussing 'Composition of Three Parts' in Playford's *Introduction to the Skill of Musick*, was less partisan and appreciated the different aims of French and Italian music: he distinguished between the needs of melody and polyphony, the warp and weft of the trio sonata texture:

When you make a *Second Treble* to a Tune, keep it always below the Upper Part, because it may not spoil the Air. But if you Compose *Sonata's* there one *Treble* has as much Predominancy as the other; and you are not tied to such a strict Rule, but one may interfere with the other, as thus: [Ex. 3 opposite]

The richness of the close-wrought trio style is beautifully com-

---

[1] *Annotazioni sopra il Compendio de' Generi, e de' Modi della Musica*, Rome, 1640.
[2] From *Roger North on Music,* edited by John Wilson.

Ex.3   Purcell

pressed into those six bars; the simple melody of the first violin's descending scale gently submerged under the rising scale accompaniment of the second violin and bass; the point of strict imitation suggested by the second, and followed by first and bass. But while the cadence is so typical of Corelli, with the third uppermost, the violin's opening melody comes directly from the English masque dance of some fifty years earlier; technical considerations must not rule out the real matter of music. In his later examples (as in his own *Sonnata's*) Purcell demonstrates the more complex forms of canonic imitation under the heading of 'Fugueing in Three Parts'; imitation by augmentation, 'recte & retro' and other convolutions end with an example of invertible writing on three subjects simultaneously, which Purcell titles modestly 'Another sort of Fugueing'. Not all composers were as adept at making ingenuity so appealing, and although canon and chaconne were two favourite sonata devices, other methods of handling the upper parts – chains of suspensions, parallel thirds and sixths, alternating bravura passage-work and antiphonal 'question and answer' – were less technically demanding, but guaranteed equality. Only as the demands of *cantabile* melody overwhelmed the requirements of polyphony did the true trio sonata texture give way to 'tune plus accompaniment' as in Sammartini (Ex. 1c), and even here the seeds of this development are found in Doni's eulogy of the violin as an essentially soloistic instrument.

The connection between texture and form in the trio sonata inevitably involves the much overemphasised division of sonatas into two categories: *da chiesa* and *da camera*. Although it might be facetious to equate this with the all-purpose claims of modern advertising – 'Suitable for the office or the home' – or the renaissance selling-line of 'Apt for Voyces or Violls', it is unnecessary to dwell too closely on the territorial distinctions of the two types. The division was most emphasised, in fact, by the French dictionary compilers after 1700, and followed up by their German imitators. Here is Sébastien de Brossard's definition of 'Sonata' and its two subdivisions from his *Dictionnaire*, first published in 1701:

Sonatas are ordinarily extended pieces, *Fantasias*, or *Preludes*, etc., *varied* by all sorts of emotions and styles, by rare or unusual chords, by simple or double Fugues, etc., etc., all purely according to the fantasy of the Composer, who, being restricted by none but the general rules of Counterpoint, nor by any fixed metre or particular rhythmic pattern, devotes his efforts to the inspiration of his talent, changes the rhythm and the scale as he sees fit, etc. One finds [sonatas] in 1, 2, 3, 4, 5, 6, 7, and 8 Parts, but ordinarily they are for *Violin alone* or for *two* different *Violins* with a *Basso continuo* for the Clavecin, and often a more *figurated* bass for the *Viola da gamba*, the *Bassoon*, etc. Thus there is an infinity of styles, but the Italians reduce them ordinarily to two types.

The first comprises the Sonatas *da chiesa* – that is, proper for the church –, which begin usually with a *grave* and *majestic* movement, suited to the dignity and sanctity of the place; after which comes some sort of gay and animated fugue, etc. Those are what are rightly known as *Sonatas*.

The second type comprises the *Sonatas* called *da Camera* – that is, proper at Court [Chambre]. These are actually suites of several little pieces suitable for dancing and composed in the same Scale or Key. Such Sonatas begin ordinarily with a *Prelude*, or little *Sonata*, which serves as a preparation for all the other [pieces]. Next come the *Allemande*, the *Pavane*, the *Courante*, and other dances or serious Airs; then come the *Gigues*, the *Passacailles*, the *Gavottes*, the *Menuets*, the *Chaconnes*, and other gay Airs; and all that composed in the same Key or Scale and played consecutively comprises a Sonata *da camera*.

In the expanded version of his definition (for the third edition of *c.*1710) Brossard enlarged on the distinction between dance movements and abstract movements ('Adagios or Largos etc. mixed with fugues that provide the Allegros'), and quoted Corelli's works as models of the two varieties. Unfortunately, Corelli's sonatas do not bear out Brossard's definitions; Op. 4 no. 10, for example, has only one dance movement, *Tempo di Gavotta* after a prelude of adagio-allegro-grave form, while Sonata 10 of the preceding *da chiesa* set is framed by an *allemanda* and *giga* in all but name.[1]

The two titles originated in Italy long before the definitions of the French, at a time when there was a real difference, both in content and intent, between 'abstract' music and 'dance' music. But with the cross-fertilisation that was inevitable when both types were published between the same covers, and in the same keys, distinctions of form and function evaporated, and the titles came to indicate a greater or lesser degree of seriousness. Tarquinio Merula had been the first to bring the two terms together in a single title in 1637 (see p. 22), and the implication would seem to have been simply that they were adaptable to all needs, since he had already described himself in 1624 as 'organista di chiesa, e di camera'. We may also note the ten *Sonate da Camera* by Antonio Veracini, published in Italy at the end of the seventeenth century, which reappeared a few years later as *Sonate da Chiesa* in Amsterdam; even Estienne Roger, the publisher, failed to see any incongruity.

By the turn of the century it would be fair to assume that any sonata of four movements (slow-fast-slow-fast) without dance titles could be listed as *da chiesa*; there would be at least one fugal movement, in general the texture would allow the bass as much contrapuntal activity as the upper parts, and weighty adagios would balance polyphonic allegros. A *da camera* listing would imply at least some of the diversional qualities of a dance suite; there would often be more than four movements, usually bi-partite with dance titles, lighter texture and less thematic use of the bass part. Counterpoint was avoided (Corelli often suppressed the third entry of a point), homophonic textures were encouraged. As might be expected, however, there are almost no examples of these perfect distinctions in practice, just as there are almost no classical sonatas that obey all the dictates of the textbook; Corelli, like Haydn, frequently falls out of line, and you are left with little more than the regularity of a Bassani or a Koželuch to demonstrate the rule. It is the mixing of the styles (both formal and national), the break-

---

[1] It seems unnecessary to assume that the papal edict of 1653 banning the use of dances and secular melodies in church had any influence on the division since Corelli, who should surely have been above suspicion, included a *Giga* in his *da chiesa* Op. 5 no. 5.

ing of the rules and the adapting of the textures that give the form its vitality; good music is rarely orthodox and Grassineau's dictionary definition of 1740 reads like a pedant's *cri de coeur* when he pleads that 'Trios are the finest kinds of composition, and ought to be nicely regular'.

The trio sonata was essentially the province of the amateur. The professional understandably preferred to shine alone in a solo sonata, although he might indulge a taste for ensemble music in private and among colleagues. It was a matter of some importance to Roger North that his brother, Lord Keeper North, who was an amateur performer on the bass-viol, 'caused the devine Purcell to bring his Itallian manner'd compositions; and with him on his harpsicord, my self another violin, wee performed them more than once, of which Mr Purcell was not a little proud, nor was it a common thing for one of his dignity to be so enterteined'. Amateurs, one deduces, would not have been found consorting with professionals off-duty. At the highest level, such chamber music was designed for the ears of the non-playing aristocracy and 'intended only to serve the private pleasures of the reigning prince or of the court'.[1] The fulsome dedications attached to published sets of trio sonatas conceal none too effectively their composers' hopes of performance in high places; but failing that, there were the gatherings of *dilettanti* and students who performed chamber music for pleasure and practice under the aegis of an *accademia,* a *Collegium Musicum* or a Philharmonick Club, where conviviality often appears to have replaced virtuosity. Niedt's account of German efforts ('. . . things did not go so smoothly but that from time to time one heard a little pig, even a full-grown sow; still . . . after every movement there was a rest of a hundred bars, during which time each player, if he cared to, sent for a glass of wine') balances North's description of less well-tempered English attempts ('. . . and so peice after peice, the time sliding away, while the masters blundered and swore in shifting places, and one might perceive that they performed ill out of spight to one and other'). In his assessment of the twelve trio sonatas by John Humphries, Sir John Hawkins gives us, albeit condescendingly, a picture of performance conditions at the opposite extreme from the Court. The sonatas

[1] From Koch's *Musikalisches Lexikon* of 1802; this must be one of the last examples of class distinction in musical forms.

are in a style somewhat above that of the common popular airs and country-dance tunes, the delight of the vulgar, and greatly beneath what might be expected from the studies of a person at all acquainted with the graces and elegancies of the Italians in their compositions for instruments. To this it must be attributed that the sonatas of Humphries were the common practice of such small proficients in harmony, as in his time were used to recreate themselves with music at alehouse clubs and places of vulgar resort in the village adjacent to London: Of these there were formerly many, in which six-pence at most was the price of admission.

By the middle of the eighteenth century, orchestral performance of trio sonatas is documented in the title of Stamitz's Op. 1 *Orchestra Trios* (*c*.1755) and by about 1770 there is the set of twelve sonatas for 'two Violins and a Bass or an Orchestra', attributed to Pergolesi.[1] However, there is some evidence that even before these overt signs, trio sonatas were played by large forces. Mattheson mentioned the uplifting effect of hearing sonatas by Corelli played in a Dutch church by a large ensemble of violins and organ, and Thurston Dart suggested that Purcell's trios may have been amplified in the same way for use in the Chapel Royal. We know from Burney (see p. 98) that Boyce's trios were performed both in the theatres and the London pleasure gardens. Presumably the violas doubled the bass line, either at the octave or unison; there seems no reason why this practice should not be restored today.[2]

The popularity of the trio as an accompaniment for cantatas and concertos must also have derived from its suitability for either single string or multiple performance; the motets of Rosenmüller, the operas and *Musiche Sacre* of Cavalli (who appears to have experienced some difficulty in writing grammatically in more than three parts anyway),[3] and the long line of English organ concertos in the eighteenth century illustrate the flexibility of the trio grouping in its pseudo-orchestral role.

While this adaptability must be held to the credit of the Italian violin, 'the best utensill of Apollo', the international spread of the trio sonata was due to the enthusiasm of itinerant Italian players coupled with the activities of Italian publishers. The Venetian firms of Gardano, Vincenti and Sala were among the first to note that an amateur market showed the best returns (professionals

[1] According to RISM, these are by Domenico Gallo.

[2] It is not impossible that *da chiesa* and *da camera* referred, in some cases, to suitability or unsuitability for mass performance.

[3] See *Cavalli* by Jane Glover (London, 1978).

wrote their own music), and even expatriate Italian composers such as Buonamente and Marini sent their music back to Venice for publication. Less scrupulous publishers followed the Italian lead: Roger and Le Cène in Amsterdam, Walsh in London, and Le Clerc and Boivin in Paris did not shrink from practising piracy in their business tactics, although their engraved works are amongst the finest products of the century. 'Thro ye art of graving etching & printing' wrote Roger North gratefully 'musick is come to great perfection, being thereby strongly propagated, much more than when all passed in MSS. wch. were not onely hard to get, but often slovenly wrote'.

Trio sonatas normally circulated in separate part-books – such curios as the three minuscule pieces by Marc'Antonio Negri published on three superimposed staves in 1611 are the exception – while solo sonatas were almost invariably printed in score. Sets of sonatas were preferred, containing from three to twelve works in each, and often arranged according to some formal pattern: key sequence determined the order of Purcell's 1683 set, Reinken alternated *da chiesa* and *da camera*, Vivaldi and Corelli each ended with a chaconne. Sonatas would often be included, almost as make-weights, in collections of vocal music; alternatively, sonatas by several composers would be gathered together to make a single instrumental set. The first published anthology of instrumental music consisted, in fact, of twelve trio sonatas issued by Monti in Bologna in 1680, and MS collections (such as that assembled by Canon Rost of Strasbourg) were even more eclectic. As a remarkable example of the speed with which such material circulated in Europe, it is worth noting that the Monti collection (plus a few works by Vitali) was copied out in England, probably by Francis North, the Lord Keeper, who died five years after the collection was first published.[1]

It is the transmission and influence of the Italian models throughout the rest of Europe that will be traced in the later chapters of this survey. Looking, for the moment, to the origins of the trio sonata, together with Roger North, 'wee cannot wonder, that among the courters of musicke, an Itallian taste should prevaile'.

---

[1] B.M. MS Add. 31436. For a listing of North's foreign repertoire see Peter Holman in *Early Music*, Vol. 6 No. 1, p. 26.

Italy

It is the exotic confection of the opera house which evokes Italian music for the modern listener – not the purely instrumental music. Transported by the sights and sounds of a Monteverdi, a Puccini or a Rossini, we find it difficult to work up an equal enthusiasm for a mere violinist and to admit Corelli to the same level of Parnassus. He is no longer the 'Orpheus of our time'; we are sceptical that the arrival of his chamber music in England 'cleared the ground of all other sorts of musick whatsoever'; and we find it hard to go along with Roger North when he declares that the sonatas 'became the onely musick relished for a long time, and there seemed to be no satiety of them, nor is the vertue of them yet exhaled, and it is a question whether it will ever be spent, for if musick can be im-mortall, Corelli's consorts will be so'. To us their immortality has become tinged with respectability, not to say tainted by the music lesson and the history book. It takes a conscious effort to reposition these works in context as the most phenomenal success of the whole baroque period: seventy-eight reprints during his own life-time (forty-eight of them in Italy) and another thirty during the next century, figures which give some idea of the way Corelli's works were 'to the musitians like the bread of life', in North's inimitable phrase.

Although the forty-eight trios of Opp. 1 to 4 are the greatest single landmark in Italian baroque music, Corelli was evolutionary, not revolutionary. There was nothing exactly new in the trios, nor anything particularly virtuoso – in fact their modest technical demands must have contributed not a little to their amazing sales. They epitomise the eighteenth-century virtues of balance, modera-tion and precision – what we might well find puritan, undemonstra-tive and predictable; we scorn the century for adding *Il Moderato* to Milton's *L'Allegro e Il Penseroso* and opt for the music that is neurotic rather than noble.

But the Corellian synthesis and refinement produced, for the first time, a vernacular for the trio sonata that was internationally accepted,[1] and, like the language of the English virginalists, capable of carrying conviction through its very phraseology. The significance of this will appear later when we consider the 'Corellians' in the international battle of styles; for the moment we

[1] The international fuss was over the Op. 5 solo sonatas, not the trios.

should think of Corelli, not as the culmination of many successful attempts at trio writing, but as the composer who balanced diverse elements from a number of different schools. For the first time, a 'school' could exist under the name of a single composer.

Italian music was powerful, but Italy, in fact, did not exist – it could be dismissed as 'a geographical expression' even in the nineteenth century. Its fortune in the mid-1600s was to possess all the ingredients of successful music-making in a large number of independent city-states, conveniently grouped together in the north. Less than 100 miles separated Cremona, the source of the newly perfected violins, from the great orchestras of Bologna; or the singers and composers of the court of Mantua from the avid publishers of Venice. Experiment at such close quarters, whether it was mutual or competitive, means that the origins of the trio sonata, its scoring and uses, are blurred today by the lack of documentation, and were to some extent in the seventeenth century by a toleration of all manner of alternatives in performance.

Disentangling the instrumental canzona from the new sonata, or allocating the *concertante* style to chamber or church is not made any easier, for instance, by such title-pages as Tarquinio Merula's *Canzoni, overo Sonate Concertate per chiesa, e camera a due et a tre* published in Venice in 1637. 'Per ogni sorti d'instrumenti' is a constant refrain, and only recent research into instrumental combinations has contradicted this appearance of permissiveness. The alternative instrumentation of 'violino o cornetto' has already been mentioned in the first chapter. It is worth remarking here that cornetti were assumed to be as agile as violins – the demands made of them in Monteverdi's *Magnificat* prove as much – since their playing technique was then an extension of recorder style rather than an adaptation of trumpet playing, as today.

Even defining a starting point for the trio sonata is somewhat arbitrary. Monteverdi provides a convenient, and plausible point of departure. In the preface to his vocal *Scherzi musicale a tre voci* of 1607, he suggested that 'the ritornelli at the end of each stanza may be played with two "violini da braccio" on the soprano lines, and a "Basso dal Chitarrone", or a harpsichord or other similar instrument on the bass'. This probably implied a continuo realisation, although both the chitarrone and the *spinetta* were quoted by Agazzari in the same year as being melodic, ornamental instru-

ments.[1] Rossi gave a similar combination for his two collections of
dance movements (1607 and 1608) – two violas or two cornetti
plus chitarrone – and Cima included two actual *Sonate* in a volume
of 'sacred concerti' of 1610.

Immediately the form is sighted, however, the hunt becomes a
matter of some complexity. Chronology is never a very good guide
to the development of a musical form, least of all in Italy where the
experiments of individual centres meant inevitable discontinuity.
Setting bounds by titling, and aiming only for those quarries called
trio sonatas (as Newman's excellent study does) means overlooking
the casual way in which the composers themselves confused sonata,
concerto and canzona. The trio sonata concept developed under
many different names. Geography helps to make the valid point
that certain districts (Mantua, Venice, Bologna, Modena, and
eventually Rome and Naples) maintained their own 'school';[2]
but their boundaries were penetrated by the spread of published
sonatas, and the travels of composers like Marini and Farina (to
Germany), Buonamente (to Warsaw) and Bertali and Valentini
(to Vienna).

We are left, then, with two lines of pursuit: the exploration of a
distinct and abstract instrumental 'idiom' and its co-traveller, the
need to maintain coherence in large-scale abstract forms. They
were common to all Italian composers, and were synthesised most
emphatically and overtly in Corelli's publications.

The experiments in idiom in the end, violinistic idiom – are the
most obvious to ear and eye, both from title-pages and from the
printed notes; they also aroused most reaction at the time (a source
of comment often of great value to the modern performer).
Francesco Rognoni, for instance, complained in 1620 that 'one
sees today many who play cornetto, violin or other instrument who
do nothing but play *passaggi* . . . ruining the canto'. Rognoni
should have been the last to complain since his own treatise, *Selve
de varii passaggi secondo l'uso moderno*, consists of endless examples of
decorative formulae which instrumentalists could apply to simple
melodic lines. However, both his volume and his complaint indicate the enthusiasm for virtuoso decoration, incorporated in the
trio sonata almost sooner than in the solo sonata – since, while the

---

[1] *Del sonare sopra 'l basso con tutti li stromenti* (1607).

[2] See, for instance, the survey of *Venetian Instrumental Music,* by Eleanor
Selfridge-Field.

Ex.4 Turini

soloist can improvise without restraint, *passaggi* with two players together have to be written out. Example 4 from Turini's sonata based on the popular song 'Tanto tempo hormai' (1621) shows typical flourishes combined with the newly popular echo effect.[1]

The gradual emancipation of the violin from these all-purpose *passaggi* and the growing preference for the string ensemble[2] can be seen in the changing requirements of the Venetian, Biagio Marini. His Op. 1, a set of mixed sonatas, sinfonias, canzonas and dances, still maintained the alternative of cornetti for violins in certain pieces despite passages like the following, which demand bowed instruments for the *tremolo* effect (a rhythmic reiteration within one bow stroke that was much imitated – cf. Buxtehude in Ex. 22a, p. 60).

Ex.5   Marini (Op. 1 no. 3)

Op. 8, published while Marini was employed in Bavaria, shows the first effects of the German virtuoso style, and has more precise variations in scoring. We find an elaborate set of variations on the *passamezzo* for two violins; a *Sonata per l'Organo è Violino ó Cornetto*, where the second treble part and bass are given to the organ (the first example in ensemble music of a written-out keyboard part); various pieces for solo violin involving *scordatura*, the abnormal tuning of the violin to facilitate chordal playing, which was a

---

[1] A feature of Bassani's trios, and hence, one suspects, of Purcell's.
[2] Traced most thoroughly in David Boyden's *History of Violin Playing*.

particularly Teutonic device (*Sonata . . . d'Inventione*); double-stopping (*Sonata per sonar con due corde*), a *Sonata senza cadenza* (i.e. written continuously without a cadence) for two violins; and even a *Sonata in Ecco,* where the two answering violins are asked to play out of sight, in imitation of Monteverdi's echo tenors in the *Magnificat.* The scoring of the sonatas in this splendid collection gives some idea of Marini's precision:

Two violins	Sonatas 1 & 4
Two violins, or *cornetti,* and continuo	Sonatas 2, 3, 5, & 13
Two *flautini,* or *cornetti,* and continuo	Sonata 6
Two violins and *chitarrone* or *arpa doppia*	Sonata 7
Two bassoons, or *tromboni grossi,* and continuo	Sonata 8
Two bassoons and continuo	Sonata 9
Violin, optional melody bass and continuo	Sonata 10
Violin, bassoon and continuo	Sonata 11
Violin, trombone (optional) and continuo	Sonata 12

Tantalisingly, seven different opus numbers following this publication are lost, and of another only the basso continuo part is known (Op. 15). These lost pieces represent a gap of thirty years. In Op. 22, the next surviving example of trio writing, the instrumentation of the sonatas is exclusively for strings; one of the trios is for *canto e basso* (No. 2), where the bass line is independent from the continuo, the remainder are for two violins. Marini is now exploiting deliberately contrasting emotional *affetti* which only violins could achieve. In the opening section of the first sonata, for example, marked *dolcemente,* the two violins merely answer each other, with the repeating note *trillo*; they then combine for the vigorous figuration of the allegro that follows. Both slow and fast passages are ideally violinistic.

Ex.6 Marini (Op. 22 no. 1)

(a)

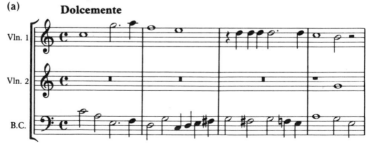

In the sonata for violin and *basso* (= violoncello), the contrast appears in the two registers used separately, as well as in the wideflung arpeggio figure which opens the *prima parte* (Marini was increasingly interested in marking the sections of his works in this way, rather than by tempo markings – a point we will return to later). Similarly, in the sonata 'sopra Fuggi dolente cori', the opening four bars are in a sostenuto style with a very slight thematic relationship to the rest of the piece, which is derived from the tune we know best as the main theme of Smetana's *Vltava* (see

Ex. 12a, p. 36). Here, however, the insistence is on abolute equality of all three parts, both in mobility and figuration. Already, in fact, devices which began as purely idiomatic features of string playing (the various *affetti*, the *passaggi* and the *tremolo*) are serving a double purpose as units of musical construction.

In addition to these techniques, which derive from the violin itself, many of the north Italian writers were drawn to the form of musical symbolism or word-painting known as *seconda prattica* to distinguish it from the earlier style when the text was subordinate to the music. For the instrumental composer this posed an intriguing dichotomy; the emotional connotations of 'mood music', which derived from a poetic impulse, were to underlie a form of essentially abstract writing (the *canzona* had long since lost any connection with a text). Monteverdi in his *Madrigals of Love and War* categorised the three basic moods as *stile concitato, stile molle* and *stile temperato*. The 'temperate' manner was already well represented in the instrumental medium, but the excited and the calm provided tempting contrasts. Marc'Antonio Negri, who had served as Monteverdi's assistant, absorbed the fanfare and battle motives of the *concitato* style into the third of his *Affetti amorosi* sonatas (1611) – the first trio sonatas to be printed in score. The ultimate extension of the technique must be the *Tiple a Tre* by the first of the Neapolitan trio composers, Andrea Falconiero; the Spanish domination of Naples accounts for its title, 'Battalla de Barabaso yerno de Satanas', and with 125 bars of alternating triple and duple fanfares it rivals the naïveté of the Spanish organ *battallas* from which it derives. Fortunately for Falconiero's reputation, there is much greater charm, and surprising rhythmic imagination in *L'Eroica, La Murroya* and the *Ciaccona* from the same collection of 1650.

Ex.7   Falconiero (La Murroya)

The obviousness of the 'battle' style guaranteed it a short but vivid career in abstract music. In the 'trumpet' school of Bologna it survived as an occasional imitative fugal subject, known as 'violino in tromba'; Purcell's D major sonata from his 1693 set (see Ex. 34a, p. 88), or Corelli's Op. 1 no. 9 show how the obviousness of this type of theme could be balanced either by a contrasted counter-subject, or, in Corelli's case, by periodic changes of mood and speed. Legrenzi, on the other hand, made this device the mainstay of several extended movements by careful manipulation of the string entries and by incorporating a repeated figure into the fanfare. In *La Bonacossa* (Op. 8 no. 9) it is an octave leap, and in *La Benaglia* (Op. 4 no. 3) a reiterated semiquaver pattern climbing up to a top A; both these subjects have a spaciousness that distinguishes the theme proper from the violinistic effect (Ex. 8 overleaf).

A similar development overtook many other tricks of the violinists' trade; what had started as an ornament, an embellishment borrowed from the vocalists, or a device of mood-setting such as Monteverdi's *stile concitato*, were either found to be lacking in potential and abandoned, or else extended into a component of musical argument. An expansion of the cadential *passaggi* shown in Ex. 4 produced the full toccata-like sections of, for example,

Ex.8 Legrenzi

(a) La Bonacossa (Op. 8 no. 9)

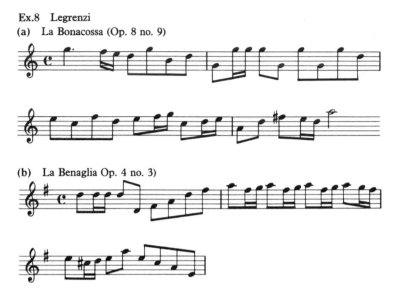

(b) La Benaglia Op. 4 no. 3)

Corelli's Op. 3 no. 12; the *tremolo* effect became, in the hands of Riccio and Gabriel Usper, the mainspring of whole sequences of harmonies, sometimes remarkably modern in their progressions, initiating a type of movement that depended entirely on harmonic expectancy and the power of suspensions. The advanced modulations of later examples (from Usper and Buonamente) resulted as much from the emphasis on texture and sonority that the *tremolo* demanded as from any intention of shocking with harmony. For the next hundred years such a texture of suspensions and resolutions in unbroken string writing would be praised for its harmony, when very often a large part of its effect was accentuated by sudden homophony. Vertical thinking, so to speak, took over in such passages from horizontal thinking.

These last extensions of the 'idiomatic' language of the trio sonata lead us into the territory of form and the control of musical shape with devices which, though they may originally have been derived from a passing embellishment, became the punctuation marks of the larger structures. Experimentation with these larger forms had also, by the middle of the seventeenth century, codified certain solutions as worth repetition and expansion, and abandoned others less amenable to inflation.

The development of trio sonata thought from the contrapuntal language of the canzona seems as confused to us as it obviously was to the original participants. Merula's ambiguous title of *Canzoni, overo sonate concertate per chiesa, e camera* is matched by Giovanni Picchi, who listed a work as *canzona* in the index and marked it *sonata* in the part-books. Merula, it is true, took over many of the initial ideas of canzona idiom (particularly the repeated note figure) but developed them with greater freedom to digress and frequently with an added touch of humour rarely present in the canzona proper. His programmatic titles appear, for once, to be related to the musical content: *La Gallina,* for example, has a subject based on the clucking of a hen, and *La Polachina* begins with the turn associated with Polish dances. Beyond this the pieces tend towards a polarisation of thought, with the two violins often moving in thirds and the *violone* gaining increasing independence from the *basso continuo* towards the end of the collection. (Merula distinguishes carefully between the various combinations possible: first the *violone* provides a continuo bass, then a divided bass and, at the end of the volume, a separate third part; see p. 9.) Another escape from the *canzona* ideal was provided in this same volume by a sonata based on the *Ruggiero* theme and a *Chiacona*.

The use of variation form, either in separate *partite* (Frescobaldi, for instance) or as continuous development over a repeating bass, started from the decorative ideas of Rognoni – the adding of *passaggi* to a simple melody – and extended through the rest of the period as a standard large-scale form encouraging the virtuoso and *concertate* style. Typical harmonic sequences were based on a series of cadence figures: the *Folia* bass, the *Bergamasca*, the *Ballo del Gran Duca,* the *Passamezzo* and the *Romanesca* can all be reduced to three or four basic chords, which become in themselves hypnotic with repetition, and also offer a solid foundation for melodic invention. In several cases it is difficult to know whether the bass came before the melody, or vice versa – the Bergamask tune is as catchy as its bass, and 'Greensleeves' is only one of several *Romanesca* melodies. Adaptations of these basic patterns account for many other baroque basses – Merula's *Chiacona* is closely related to Monteverdi's setting of *Zefiro Torna* for two tenors (1614); both their bass lines are rhythmically adapted versions of the *Ballo del Gran Duca.* Ex. 9 shows portions of the two trio settings (the Monteverdi example has been transposed up a fourth, and the note values halved):

Ex.9

(a) Monteverdi

(b) Merula

Similar sets of variations can be found in other early Italian sets of trios: Rossi employed *Ruggiero* and *Romanesca* basses in his collections of '*varie Sonate, Sinfonie, Gagliarde, Brandi, e Corrente*' (each reprinted twice by 1642); Buonamente the *Gran Duca* in his 1626 set; and Uccellini, the most persistent variation writer, offered an *Aria sopra la Bergamasca* along with eight other sets of variations in 1642. The *Folia bass* took longer to develop its popularity (Frescobaldi's keyboard variations with this title employ quite different harmonies), and we wait until Corelli's Op. 5 and Vivaldi's Op. 1 to find the full treatment of this bass.

Ex.10

(a) Il ballo del Gran Duca

(b) Passamezzo antico

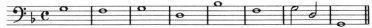

(c) Passamezzo moderno

(d) Romanesca

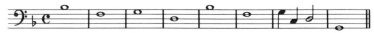

(e) Folia

(f) Ruggiero

One alternative to the cadential bass patterns which became popular towards the middle of the century, particularly for operatic laments, was a simple descending scale, usually of four notes and sometimes with a cadence tagged on to the end (see Ex. 11 below). Corelli (Op. 2 no. 12) and Purcell (Sonata VI, 1697) both employed this pattern, Corelli with a decorated bass line, and a dip into the minor, Purcell with a curious five-bar repeating pattern. More theatrical than this is the use of the form as the final movement of Cavalli's *Canzona a 3*, with fine independent bass writing in the fast fugal sections. In the tradition of Venetian opera, though hardly usual in instrumental music, the fugue is followed by an operatic lament with a broken melody that must have carried its listeners back to the final moments of *Poppea* or *L'Egisto*.

Ex.11   Cavalli

Using variation and chaconne was only one way to break the format of the canzona. Several others were available which also aimed at creating a continuity of shape in contrast to the variety of motif that the canzona encouraged. Buonamente, for instance, opened his seventh book of sonatas with one dedicated to Monteverdi in which the two violins play in canon throughout – a tricky feat when it comes to various *passaggi* which must work both as solos and in thirds. G. M. Bononcini (Op. 3), Uccellini and Cazzati also turned to canonic writing as a formal and technical challenge. Marini's *Sonata senza cadenze* mentioned earlier displayed extreme devotion to continuity, but his trios based on familiar melodies such as *La Monicha* (*La Nonette* to the French, or e.g. *The Queen's Alman* by Byrd to the English) and *Fugge dolente core* ('Vltava' to the twentieth century) offered thematic unity of an instantly recognisable kind. It was clearly assumed that the listener would be familiar with the original melody. In *Fugge dolente core,* for instance, Marini offered a closely argued section of imitative points taken from the first five notes of the melody, with inversions and stretti to complicate the issue (Ex. 12a). Then, by lopping the fifth note from the rising theme, he arrived at the material for the triple section, over which he set the original melody (Ex. 12b); and rounded off the piece with seven bars in common time, returning to the 'walking-bass' pattern of the first section.

Ex.12 Marini
(a)

Ex.13 Legrenzi

(a)

(b)

Other than a slight change of pulse there is not intended to be a noticeable jolt between the **C** and $3/1$ sections of this sonata. Indeed, the theory of the sectionalised sonata is supported far more by differences of notation apparent to the eye than by the negligible effect on the ear when changes of pulse are related proportionally to each other (the quavers of Ex. 12a, for instance, equal the minims of Ex. 12b). Even such markings as *allegro* or *adagio* were frequently added merely to confirm what the notation already implied – that, for instance, semiquavers were expected to sound fast, and semibreves slow in a movement when the tempo was unchanging. In a century brought up on dancing and dance metres, a proportional change of tempo would have given as strong a feeling of unity as a melodic link; only when the basic pulse faltered would a demarcation of material have been suspected.

The presence of dance metres in the triple sections of these sonatas carried on the long-established tradition of related tempi such as existed between pavan and galliard. The random association of dance movements in collections of sonatas was probably to encourage their sale for domestic entertaining, but it meant the continual chance of cross-fertilisation. Legrenzi, one of the most individual melodists of the Venetian school, published sonatas *da camera*, a title merely indicating that the piece was a single movement introduction to be used at the head of a sequence of dance music chosen from the samples that followed. Every one of his *da chiesa* sonatas contains at least one section in dance metre: Ex. 13a (from Op. 4 no. 1) is a *corrente*, Ex. 13b (from the end of Op. 8 no. 8) a concluding *giga*. A contrast to these dance sections was provided by the intervening fugal sections, usually on vigorous and memorable themes (see Ex. 8, p. 30), but even here the dance element can intervene: Ex. 13c (p. 40), the opening subject of *La Rossetta* (Op. 8 no. 7), is in the rhythm, though not the predictable phrase lengths, of a gigue or *canaries*.

Still more of the dance can be found in the trios of G. B. Vitali; he not only used all the traditional metres in his *Sonate da camera,* but added the newest arrivals from France, the minuet and the bourrée. As an example of the reversal of the expected flow of ideas, it is interesting to notice there had been a steady trickle of Lullian influence into Italy, particularly at the courts of Modena and Parma. Uccellini wrote 'corrente alla francese', and Bononcini introduced the gavotte into the trio sonata (1666). By 1684, Vitali

(b)

(c)

even distinguished sonatas 'alla francese, & all'Itagliana'. It is clear, though, both in Vitali's sonatas and in those of most of his contemporaries, that an absence of dance title did not mean an absence of dance influence; as a natural counterbalance to the fugue, both in predictability and sonority, the homophonic dance style was invaluable.

'Corelli,' Burney said, 'was not the inventor of his own favourite style, though it was greatly polished and perfected by him.'

Having accumulated the ingredients of the Corellian synthesis, it is straightforward enough to point out which techniques he selected to work with, and which were passed over. It is much more difficult, however, to explain the spiritual broadening which was identified in these works as soon as they appeared in print. Their qualities of refinement and moderation do not account entirely for the immediate certainty that 'if musick can be imortall, Corelli's consorts will be so', nor do they explain how Sir John Hawkins, nearly a century later, could declare that 'His music is the language of nature. . . . Men remembered and would refer to passages in it as to a classic author.'

Hawkins added a comment which conveys an extra degree of proportion and balance to Corelli's achievement; the fact that 'his compositions . . . are equally intelligible to the learned and unlearned' implies that the performer and the listener derived equal pleasure from them. Too many earlier works were solely for the delight of those playing them, and Corelli revealed a new plane of abstract musical creation in chamber terms.

The forty-eight trio sonatas had no option of alternative instrumentation. Corelli's demands were modest, and accurately indicated; the two sets of *da chiesa* sonatas (Opp. 1 and 3) call for two violins plus *Violone o Arcileuto, col Basso per l'Organo,* where the *da camera* works ask for *Violone, o Cimbalo.* While the distinction between the content of the two styles may be vague, the indications for scoring are specific, particularly the suggestion that the archlute be employed as an alternative to the melodic bass, not to the organ. (Here one must always bear in mind the Italian use of *organo* as a generic term for anything with a keyboard.)

Corelli lived in Rome in an atmosphere of peace and security that few other composers ever achieved; he was, by all accounts, a mild man, not over-generous, given to collecting pictures and dressing in black (according to Handel). His works were only published after the utmost refining and reworking, and after they had been thoroughly tested in performance – his concerti, in fact, were being played more than twenty years before they appeared in print.[1] This in itself sets his trios apart from their contemporaries;

---

[1] One criticism of Corelli's technical skill came (indirectly) from the com-

not that they lack the bursts of spontaneous virtuosity, the real violinistic *affetti*, but these sections are pruned with a cool critical eye and related to their context. The arpeggio figurations of Op. 3 no. 12, for instance, ideal as they are for the violins, do not take the licence of continuing beyond the smallest number of bars the music required for variety. Similarly, the slow sequences of suspended harmony which so delighted the eighteenth century take no bizarre turns, nor indulge in enharmonic tricks. Those piquant twists that we relish in Purcell's similar sequences today were considered a fault by Roger North, because they hindered the freedom and flow of the harmonic train of thought; they were 'short in the elegances one would expect from such studied passages'. Corelli's were indeed sonatas 'studiosi e osservati', and though an index of their devices would be a short one, as Burney said, the expected mannerisms were apportioned with an exact effect in mind. The placing of the 7/5 chord, for instance, in the penultimate bar of Ex. 14 is deliberately on the weakest beat of the bar; the harmonic sequence would be complete without it, but the rhythm would not. Corelli chose an interesting but not bizarre chromatic chord for the occasion, and fitting it unobtrusively into the flay of the parts, achieved a result which is noble rather than tortured.

Ex.14   Corelli (Op. 3 no. 12)

poser Colonna, in Bologna, who picked out what he considered to be a sequence of consecutive fifths in the *Allemanda* of Op. 2 no. 3 (see Ex. 1b, p. 7, for the offending passage). The composer was informed by letter, and sent back a very tart reply explaining the correctness of his notation ('for those who are in the dark'), but a polemical correspondence continued, with much publicity, until Colonna's death ten years later. A summary of the case is in Pincherle's *Corelli, His Life, His Work* (pp. 47–51), but Corelli's argument was that the crochets in the bass were assumed to be implicit in the following quaver rest, and thus the offending fifths would be separated by an extra harmony.

In his eagerness to locate 'pathetic and impassioned melody and modulation', Burney overlooked the purity and simplicity of Corelli's slow movements. Similarly, other contemporaries noted a lack of melodic inventiveness in some of the sonatas, a 'want of air', but failed to observe that Corelli was actually refining the established principles of thematic unity. The simple thematic relationship between the two sections of Marini's sonata in Ex. 12 was expanded by Corelli in, for instance, his Op. 3 no. 2, where all four movements use the same motif. The pulse varies from expansive common time in the first movement, with the maximum number of passing notes in the 'walking-bass', to the quickening of harmonic rhythm provided by more frequent discords of the third movement. In the fugal movements there is a contrast between the severe line of the first *allegro*, which has the two violins at odds with each other in minims and contradictory quavers, and the cheerful gigue-like finale, where the violins hunt as a pair (Ex. 15 overleaf).

Ex.15 Corelli (Op. 3 no. 2)

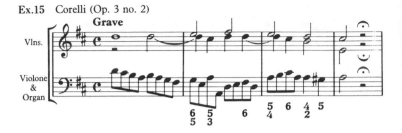

Several particularly Corellian solutions can be found even in these detached fragments. The most obvious innovation is that every movement is related; pairing of slow and fast movements had been common, but four tempi pivoting on one melodic tag was a still broader coherence. The element of variation is there, taken over from his predecessors, though it is subservient to the musical individuality of each section. The implicit rivalry between bass and treble is stated in the first movement with the most imitated of all Corelli's mannerisms, the sequence of suspensions above a 'walking-bass' in quavers; in the fugal movements the parts display more equality (the *violone* divides from the organ bass in the last movement to imitate the violins more exactly), and with the united effect of a cadential echo to both the third and fourth movements the resolution of tensions is complete.

As an antidote to such a clinical assessment in the modern manner, the same sequence of thought can be found in the more evocative terminology of Roger North which presents us with a distillation of the figures of thought that occupied the baroque mind in the analysis and valuation of just such a trio:

The entrance is usually with all the fullness of harmony figurated and adorned that the master at that time could contrive, and this is termed *Grave*. This *Grave* most aptly represents seriousness and thought. The movement is as of one so disposed, and if he were to speak, his utterance would be according, and his matter rationall and arguing. The upper parts onely fulfill the harmony, without any singularity in the movement; but all joyne in a comon tendency to provoke in the hearers a series of thinking according as the air invites, whether Magnifick or Querolous, which the sharp or flat key determines. When there hath bin enough of this, which if it be good will not be very soon, variety enters, and the parts fall into action, and move quick; and the entrance of this denouement is with a *fuge*. This hath a cast of buisness or debate, of which the melodious point is made the subject; and accordingly it is wrought over and under till, like waves upon water, it is spent and vanisheth, leaving the musick to proceed smoothly, and as if it were satisfyed and contented. After this comes properly in the *Adagio*, which is a laying all affaires aside, and lolling in a sweet repose: which state the musick represents by a most tranquill but full harmony, and dying gradually, as one that falls asleep. After this is over Action is resumed, and the various humours of men diverting themselves (and even their facetiousness and witt) are represented, as the master's fancy at that time invites, wherein the instrument or ingredient of the connexion with humane life is the measure; as a *Gavott*, which is an old French dance; and so *Minuets, Courants*, and other dancing expressions. There is often the *Andante*, and divers imitations of men's humours well knowne to the performers, so need not be described, and for the most part concluding with a *Gigue* which is like men (half foxed) dancing for joy, and so good night.

North included in his scheme not only the four regular movements of Corelli's sonatas Opp. 1 and 3, but also the dance movements of Opp. 2 and 4. These trios are composed on less regular patterns with deliberately less building-up of expectancy. A *Preludio* opens each work with a display, often of alternating moods and techniques; there are more movements in the dotted rhythms of French ballet (especially the *Allemandas*), and less insistence on fair shares for all – in Op. 4 the *Corrente* of No. 3, for example, and the *Giga* of No. 7 are first violin solos accompanied by the other parts. There is imitation without fugues, an infrequent use of *affetti* (the chromatic *adagio* of the first sonata in Op. 4 stands out for its *tremolo*), and a general reluctance to discuss more than one idea per movement. This in itself is a feature of the dance although the effective dance element is minimal.[1] The abstract, instrumental qualities of dance music reside in its rhythmic gestures, its even pacing, its anticipatory upbeats, and its lack of involvement with melody. Corelli stripped these features of any theatrical element, and investigated them with an insistence that Brossard would have termed 'perfidia' – 'always following the same design, the same melody, the same passage, the same figuration'.

The opposite characteristic, 'stravaganza', was never part of Corelli's make-up: it was this restraint, and his unwillingness to impose novelty or surprise on the listener, that made him the ideal model for his contemporaries. The fact that 'all the varieties of Corelli's harmony, modulation, and melody, might perhaps be comprised in a narrow compass'[2] made him an easy target for imitators, either patent or clandestine. The activities of various 'Corellians' will feature in later chapters, but the works of Ravenscroft deserve mention here for their chequered career, as well as their imitative workmanship. Although all twelve of Ravenscroft's sonatas were published in 1695 in Rome (where he may well have

[1] Op. 4 no. 10, for instance, includes a *Preludio* of several sections, a *Grave*, and a single dance movement, *Tempo di Gavotta,* which is totally undanceable.
[2] Burney, *op. cit.*

been a pupil of Corelli), two of them were later attributed to Caldara, and another nine were published in Paris as Corelli's Op. 7. As test-cases of what was considered ideally Corellian they may be placed alongside the trios by James (alias Giacomo) Sherard, a London apothecary; and the excellent sonatas for two recorders and basso continuo by William Corbett (who divided his time between music and the secret service) – to name but the English branch of the Corelli factory. Sherard, a botanist, as well as chemist, offered a charming apologia for his imitations of the 'Italian Musick'. Admitting a disparity between his product and the originals 'as betwixt their fruits, and such as we raise from their Stocks', he asks that we 'make allowances for the differences of Soil, and Climate, and not wholly blame the industry of the Planter'. Like Ravenscroft and Corbett, Sherard found the poise of the true Corellian adagio most difficult to achieve, although these movements with their long chains of suspensions were obviously a prime feature for imitation; fugal subjects tended to be longer than Corelli's wonderfully compact themes, and the discourse correspondingly more garrulous. Ravenscroft also over-indulged the echo effect during the course of a movement to give added finality to a cadence.

Dom Antonio Eximeno, the Italian equivalent of Charles Burney, recommended four features of Corelli's works to the attention of later composers – 'the variety of beautiful and well worked out [fugal] subjects, the exact observance of the laws of harmony, the firmness of the basses, [and] the fitness for exercising the hands of the performer'. There may be more 'original' examples of any one of these virtues both before and after Corelli, but no other writer combined the four with such felicity and frequency. It is overstating the case to claim that Corelli's originality lay in his not having any, but it is true that only one person was allowed the privilege of halting the march of progress and surveying the conquered territory, selecting and exploiting those areas that had been annexed. There is a limit to the amount of polishing and refinement that the pressures of commercial music allow (then as now); and in the concerto-infected atmosphere of Italy in the early 1700s, the more audacious scale of orchestral music and the increasing emphasis on the bravura element in the idiom of the violin combined to lure the trio sonata onwards from its moment of consolidation.

Corelli's works stood as a counsel of perfection not of progress. Less perfected tendencies already hinted at in the works of his contemporaries proved to be catalysts for further exploration. Mazzaferrata for example, in his twelve trios of 1674, offered four-movement works, with the slower harmonic movement and the less earnest counterpoint that became the hallmark of the late baroque manner. The extended figuration of Bassani's Op. 5 (1683, and three reprints) attempted a length of phrase capable of sustaining the listener's interest only when combined with the expansion of range and chromaticism that came after 1700; too frequently the allegros merely mark time to the violin repeating itself in semiquavers.

Corelli, the ultimate in the distilled, 'intensive' style, was a dead-end; the 'extensive' style meant the incorporation of at least one new ingredient into a perfect recipe. To remove a card from the Corellian house was impossible, but a skilled hand might add one storey.

It was the injection of the concerto confidence into Vivaldi's trios that set them apart from most rivals – Albinoni and dall'Abaco excepted. Vivaldi revealed the raw materials of baroque construction which draw their strength from the concerto sonority rather than the sonata; the sequence, the arpeggio figuration, the pedal-point, the reiterated units of rhythm. They find their most enthusiastic advocates nowadays amongst the 'unlearned' rather than the 'learned', to apply John Hawkins' test. But the Vivaldian synthesis is not one of nobility and refinement; instead it is the infusion of energy and boldness into the traditional sonata. There is more sophistication in his treatment of small-scale forms than in many of his unpublished concertos. The concentration of *concertante* devices without the solo/tutti contrast produced a broadening of language without over-inflating the dimensions of the trio.

Vivaldi's first publication, in 1705, was a set of twelve trios, and an additional two sonatas appeared as part of Op. 5 in 1716. The scoring of these, and most of his unpublished sonatas, is for two violins and basso continuo; two flutes, two oboes, violin and cello, flute and violin, recorder and bassoon make up the other scorings RV 80–86[1]). The two 'trios' for lute, violin and continuo (RV 82 and

---

[1] The traditional confusion over Vivaldi numbering has been resolved by the catalogue of Peter Ryom (RV).

85) are anomalies, since both lute and violin play the same part throughout. As an experiment in sonority they can be taken to represent one of Vivaldi's strongest interests, but it is more probable that the two upper parts are alternatives.

In the Op. 1 trios experimentation with texture produced effects which relate to the concerto style and have no counterpart in Corelli. Ex. 16a is typical Vivaldian *perfidia*; texture and harmony are left to themselves, providing the essential nature of the violin is being fulfilled – the hallmark of the concerto thinker. Even when the layout appears to relate rather more closely to the Corellian model (as in Ex. 16b) a concerto element is added by the cross-string jumps of the first violin contradicting the serenity of the walking-bass.

This cultivation of tensions within the instrumental grouping produces a divorce between top and bottom in many of the dance movements. The *Corrente* of Sonata No. 2 is a dialogue between the two violins, with rudimentary support from the bass, while the

Ex.16   Vivaldi (Op. 1 no. 7)

(a)

(b) **Andante**

propulsion of the *Grave* of Sonata No. 8 comes from the dotted rhythm of the continuo (very similar to tutti passages in the Op. 3 and Op. 4 concerti) above which the violins discuss totally different topics. The unifying agent in this scheme of tensions was not a thematic one, as it had been with Corelli, but harmonic. Only one sonata (No. 12) is actually constructed over a chaconne bass (*Folia*), but the chain of predictable, often wide-stepping, harmonies employed so frequently in the other sonatas induces a sensation of familiarity which takes the place of thematic unity. (The harmonic sequence in the *Capriccio* of Sonata No. 1 is precariously close to that of the last of Paganini's *Caprices* for solo violin – the basis for so many variations.) The only drawback to this solution is the undue emphasis it placed on cadences and cadential formulae. In the concertos these were disguised by tutti entries, but in the sonatas Vivaldi fell back on the weaker device of echo effects and the trick of continuing the violin figuration after the final harmony has been reached (Sonata No. 8, *Giga*, for instance, or the *Corrente* of Sonata No. 9).

Eventually the tension of instrumental grouping was resolved by increasing the solo-concerto element in the sonatas. This is most obvious in the second half of the Op. 1 set where the predominance of the first violin, and the co-operation of the second violin and bass as subsidiary accompanists mark the beginning of a rococo polarisation which favoured melody more than the interplay of equal parts.

Vivaldi's trio sonatas carefully avoid the fugal possibilities of the medium (as do his concertos), and the knack of devising characterful and vigorous subjects which we noted in Legrenzi seems to have passed to Albinoni, 'Musico do violino dilettante veneto' as he described himself. Bach's borrowing of fugue subjects from Albinoni's Op. 1 trio sonatas (see p. 64) are sufficient commendation, but in later publications Albinoni's enjoyment of extremes led to such contrapuntal experiments as Op. 8, where two of the three voices in each fugue are in strict canon. Against these flights of technical fancy was balanced the more openly emotional style of his slow movements, where definite anguish, mingled with a delight in the sheer sonority to be achieved from the interlocking of the violin parts, replaced the restraint of Corelli. More than the small gap of ten years seems to separate the almost slavishly Corellian opening of Op. 1 no. 10 from the harmonic interweaving of Op. 8 no. 4 (a close relative of the Sixth Brandenburg Concerto?) – Ex. 17.

The preoccupation with ensemble sonorities, also a feature of Vivaldi's thinking, naturally found an easier outlet in concerto writing, but the intensity of Albinoni's lyrical style, with his almost operatic use of rests to break up a melodic line, had a more effective place in his solo sonatas.

The true trio layout was ideal territory for the less 'progressive' writer. The close-knit imitations of a Caldara, for example, in his Op. 1 or the long-spun melodic lines (usually for the first violin) in Bonporti's four sets of trios placed no strain on the normal number and layout of movements, but tell us very little that is new about the medium. Almost as a by-product of these two extremes a new intimacy and gentleness became associated with the trio sonata which we do not find in either the full concerto or the virtuoso solo sonata. The trios of Tartini, for instance, compared with his more publicised solo sonatas, have a lightness of touch which includes the reduction of a three-movement form to a simple two move-

Ex.17 Albinoni (Op. 8 no. 4)

ments, and a preference for utilising the two violins as an alternative to a single violin in double-stopping (Ex. 18 overleaf).

Tartini, after Corelli the most formative violin teacher of the century in Italy, is also one of the modern string player's best sources of information on performance practice. His exhaustive *Traité des agrémens* (until recently only the French translation was known) is balanced by a delightful *Letter* to a young lady advising her on basic violin technique (translated into English by Dr Burney):[1]

You should make yourself a perfect mistress in every situation and part of the bow, as well in the middle as at the extremities.... When you are a perfect mistress of this part of a good performer, a swell will be very easy to you; beginning with the most minute softness, encreasing the tone to its loudest degree, and diminishing it to the same point of softness with which you began, and all this in the same stroke of the bow.

[1] *A Letter from the late Signor Tartini to Signora Maddalene Lombardini . . . published as an important lesson to performers on the violin* (London, 1771).

Ex.18 Tartini (Op. 3 no. 2)

Tartini's views on violin playing coloured the Italian approach to the *galant* idiom of the north, and the finesse of his notation matched the intricacies of either French or German mannered music of this sensual period. But with the warmth of expression and eloquence of line that he advocated came a negation of the traditional tensions of the Italian trio sonata; it was not a style of performance that crossed frontiers with the same ease that Corelli's works had been transmitted some fifty years earlier. The idiom had overwhelmed the form. Even the title that Tartini gave his violin academy in Padua – 'The School of Nations' – announced that he was promoting an international *player's* vocabulary taking the place of the vernacular *composer's* idiom that Corelli had offered.

But, as we shall see, it was the progress of the Corellian ideal around Europe that marked the true triumph of the trio sonata outside its homeland. The 'spice of Italy' was in constant demand.

Modern preoccupation with the culmination of an art-form – the aesthetic equivalent of 'the Greatest Hits' policy – has produced some curious anomalies in the territory of the trio sonata. Those pinnacles of the High Baroque – Bach, Handel, Scarlatti, Vivaldi, all of them bestsellers – appear to have reacted hardly at all to the most popular chamber form of their time. Consequently, with that peculiar inversion of logic that attends 'popularity', we (the public) have more or less ignored the presence of the trio sonata outside Italy.

After all, Bach wrote a mere five (the organ trios slip our mind) and three of those are not authentic. Sonatas amount to very few pages in the complete works of Handel, and at least half of his trios are made from material probably adapted by his publisher from other works. Scarlatti never rose to the form at all; Vivaldi's single published set are far from his best pieces, and *La Folia* is the only one we would recognise. The popularity poll registers almost nil. Even in the lower echelons, who knows a trio sonata by Purcell that is not the 'Golden' or one by Telemann that *doesn't* include the recorder? Even statistics are incapable of improving the situation; the percentage of complete works occupied by trio sonatas (even counting the *St Matthew Passion* or *Messiah* as one work) gives the following dismal table:

Bach	0·7%
Handel	1·7%
Scarlatti	0·0%
Vivaldi	3·6%
Purcell	2·6%

When Corelli comes out at 66% (all in print during his lifetime), Cazzati at 44% and Vitali at 86%, the trio texture is seen to be almost exclusively the preoccupation of the 'most fam'd Italian masters'.

Venetian and Roman publishers take much of the credit for disseminating the style outside Italy, and Vienna, the nearest foreign centre, was already feeling the effects of the first wave of Italian players and composers in the early part of the seventeenth century. The debilitating effect of the Thirty Years War encouraged the less expensive musical undertakings, and the sudden rash of trio writing in Southern Germany may even have been directly related to the condition of the Habsburg coffers.

Our best early source for the state of trio sonatas outside Italy is a set of three manuscript part-books assembled by a Strasbourg curate, François Rost (and later acquired by Brossard, cf. p. 108), containing, in Brossard's words, 'a most curious collection of at least 151 sonatas, allemandes, fantasias and other pieces composed by the most illustrious authors who flourished around the middle of the past century – that is from about 1640 to 1688'. Out of the 150 numbered pieces, only twenty-seven are not scored for two violins and basso continuo – the part-book is marked 'Organo'. Many of the pieces are anonymous but among the Italians mentioned are Valentini, Bertali (both in Imperial service in Vienna), Nicholai, Cazzati and Vitali. Schmelzer leads the transalpine contingent (as befits a nobleman) with fifteen sonatas; followed by Kerll, Rosenmüller and Clamor Heinrich Abel, the splendidly named grandfather of the eighteenth-century gamba virtuoso. Against the modern disparagement of anthologies, this collection gives a remarkably complete cross-section of enterprising and, for the period, modern works. Omissions include composers who ignored the trio sonata in favour of either solo or concerto forms (Biber,[1] Muffat, Strunck), some who scored their trios for combinations that were not of interest to Rost (Kühnel's works for two bass viols, for instance) and others who were simply too distant to be known to him (Buxtehude).

Of the Italians, Cazzati is mentioned elsewhere (pp. 81, 86), Valentini is adventurous only in his dynamic markings – he is the first to use p, pp and even ppp – and Bertali alone stands out as 'Valoroso nel Violino'[2] with a real grasp of the *concertante* use of two violins and the triadic sonorities that suit them so well – Ex. 19.

Alessandro Poglietti, a bizarre virtuoso who became Imperial organist, is best remembered today for his programmatic keyboard suites which favour military scenes. Even his strange trio sonata, scored for cornetto, 'flauto' (= recorder), bassoon and organ continuo, is over-enthusiastic with its fanfare effects; the cornetto part is entirely playable on the natural trumpet. Ironically, Poglietti was killed in the Turkish siege of Vienna in 1683.

---

[1] Although Biber's *Harmonia artificiosa-ariosa* (seven *Partias* for *scordatura* violins and continuo, *c*.1686) would surely have deserved inclusion.

[2] A compliment from his compatriot, Bertoli, in 1645.

Ex.19 Bertali (Sonata 'Taussent Gulden')

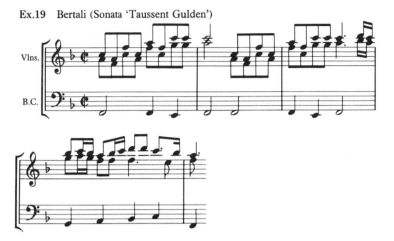

Schmelzer was the first German to oust Italians from the position of Imperial *Hofkapellmeister,* partly by sheer virtue of his skill as a violinist, and partly for his partiality to rich and varied scoring suitable for ceremonial purposes (a purpose for which Bertali's fanfare pieces were also suited). Almost half his sonata output is trio writing, although he favoured the violin, viola da gamba and continuo grouping rather than the characteristic Italian grouping of two violins and bass. The scale of each section of his sonatas is increased from their Italian models, partly to accommodate expansive and florid solo writing for each instrument. Such passages as Ex. 20 overleaf obviously derive from solo violin sonatas, and when repeated almost note for note by the gamba merely hold up the progress of the movement. Italian influence shows itself in some repeated devices. For example, his passages in thirds, usually in dotted rhythm, and his written-out accelerating trills (beginning on the lower note) are identical with Monteverdi's ornamental style for cornetti or violins (cf. also Buxtehude, in Ex. 22b, p. 61–2).

In spite of the frequent suggestions for alternative scoring that we find in the larger-scale German pieces (trombone or bassoon, for instance, in place of the string bass, and cornetti and trombones replaceable by violins and violas in Pezel's *Hora Decima*), instrumentation of the trio sonata remained unadventurous. Only later, and farther north, did the German predilection for wind instruments

Ex.20   Schmelzer (Son. IV, 1672)

show itself, unless we follow the instructions of Georg Muffat (quoted on p. 13) to their extreme, and reduce his concerto scoring to its minimum. It is perfectly practical, he said, to play several of his *concerti grossi* with the three *concertino* parts alone; it is less clear whether he really intended the 'musicians who can play and control the French oboe or shawm agreeably' and the 'good bassoon player' to undertake the same task without the support of the *ripieno* orchestra, though it would be an experiment worth making either on his own or contemporary concertos.

Krieger, also represented in the Rost anthology, is remarkable not for his trios themselves as much as his thoughtfulness, unique for the time, in publishing his sonatas separately. Having obviously suffered from carrying around other people's sets of six or twelve, he suggested that his arrangement would make it easier when only one sonata was required as dinner music for a prince, or as a contribution to an amateur musical evening. His contemporary Kühnel (see p. 85) offered a more musically inspired convenience with his remarkable trio sonatas for two *viole da gamba*, which are so written that one or the other viol always supplies a suitable bass, so making the continuo line expendable. His idiomatic scoring suggests that he was familiar with, and was probably trying to outdo, French models, although he avoided the intricacies of French ornamentation by using only the apostrophe, 'to be interpreted with any embellishment the amateur thinks fit' (Ex. 21).

As one moves towards North Germany, the partiality for including at least one viola da gamba in the trio scoring increases; the outstanding examples of this scoring are the two sets of trios, Opp. 1 and 2, by Buxtehude, both published in 1696 when he was organist of the Marienkirche in Lübeck.[1] Although the Lutheran church never made any call for the *sonata da chiesa* in its literal use, Buxtehude must have had this purpose in mind when he called them '*appropriate for church and Tafel-musik*'.[2] Even in their moments of wildest extravagance – and real virtuosity is certainly required from both players – they never forsake the calculated emotionalism that we associate with the organ music of North Germany. Such expressive devices as the chromaticism of Ex. 22a, overleaf, which would not be out of place in a setting of the Passion, is used as a

[1] They were not his first publications, so the choice of numbering is curious.
[2] Cf. Biber's *Sonatae tam aris quam aulis servientes* of 1676 ('appropriate to the altar or the court').

Ex.21 Kühnel (Son. 3)

repeated formal idea in the sonata. There are no signs that Buxtehude was familiar with Corelli's sonata planning, but his sections of fantasy and quasi-recitative for the gamba as well as the violin suggest that he knew of similar exploits in Legrenzi's church sonatas (Ex. 22b).

Ex.22 Buxtehude (Op. 1 no. 3)
(a)

Ex.22

(b) Buxtehude (Op. 2, no. 3)

First contact with Bach is made, after traversing the country from south to north, with the *Hortus Musicus* sonatas (*c.*1688) of Johann Reinken in Hamburg. Bach's free keyboard arrangements of movements from this set have failed to ensure their longevity, even though as with the Vivaldi arrangements the originals of these works are more compelling and less over-wrought than Bach's adaptations. Bach's interest must have been aroused by the scope Reinken's sonatas offered for (not entirely appropriate) Italianiate embellishing, as well as by the combination of sonata and dance suite (or, as he would have termed them in his solo violin music,

sonata and partita). Reinken gave coherence to this large-scale
scheme by drawing thematic relationships between the beginnings
of many movements; an element which Bach ignored when he
combined three different sonatas in his keyboard versions (BWV 965
and 966). Without being able to demonstrate here how Reinken's
fugal invention was expanded and improved by Bach's insertion of
extended episodes, a juxtaposition of the opening of the A minor
sonata in both versions indicates the extent of the ornamental
additions. It also, incidentally, raises the performance question of
whether the speed that is right for the Bach might not be too slow
for the Reinken.

Ex.23

There is more evidence than these works alone that Bach was familiar with sets of trio sonatas in the 'normal' scoring. Corelli's Op. 3 provided two fugal movements for expansion as BWV 579 (the B minor organ fugue, from Op. 3 no. 4) and the A major fugue in Book I of the '48' (related to Op. 3 no. 12). Albinoni's Op. 1 served the same purpose and appears to have been quarried for fugal subjects for Bach's pupils, if the two versions of BWV 951 are taken to be schoolroom exercise and master's improvement. But fugal movements are the least idiomatic form of trio writing from which to borrow. Interesting, although merely tangential to a discussion of the Bach canon, is an anonymous adaptation of

Couperin's Rondeau from *L'Impériale,* listed by Schmieder as BWV 587; even its retitling, as *Aria,* underlines the German preference for the more Italianate aspect of French music.[1] Notice also the fluency expected from the feet – an essential accomplishment if real trio writing is to be transferred to the organ:

Ex.24   Couperin (arr. ?)

Bach's set of six 'organ' trio sonatas are the logical outcome not only of his own experiments in arrangement and the German proficiency in pedal technique, but also of his teaching needs.

The title of 'a 2 Clav. e Pedal' can include the pedal clavichord as well as the organ, both of them suitable instruments for the tuition of Wilhelm Friedemann for whom the set was probably compiled between 1727 and 1729. Only the last of the six seems to have been written expressly for this purpose; the first five are in whole or in part arrangements from earlier, mostly keyboard pieces by Bach. The opening movement of Sonata No. 4 from the Sinfonia to Part II of *Cantata 76* with its tellingly contrasted scoring of oboe d'amore, viola da gamba and continuo has an adagio introduction to the Vivace; none of the other sonatas break the fast-slow-fast pattern. The slow movement of no. 3 (the most

---

[1] The Italian trend seemed a positive threat to one aristocratic lady who exclaimed at an early performance of the *St Matthew Passion*: 'God help us, my children! It's just as if one were at a comic opera' (reported by Gerber, 1732).

galant movement of the whole set) turns up again as the slow movement of the *Triple Concerto* (BWV 1044) where the addition of a *pizzicato* part converts it into the quartet form that Quantz considered the real test of a composer.[1] Mozart's reworking of this same movement, for violin, viola and cello (K 404a), re-emphasises Bach's preference for a more equidistant layout of voices than the SSB scoring of the Italians would allow. The upper parts of all the trios frequently dip below the bottom G of the violin, and the wide-ranging bass lines are, in many cases, unsuitable for either cello or gamba. Mozart chose his movement well.

In his trios, Bach preferred a tonal contrast between his upper parts which 'normal' scoring did not offer,[2] and, once the movement is set in motion, a continuity of sonority and interplay which would tax the wind or string player. There are virtually no rests in either of the two upper parts of the *Allegro* that opens the E flat sonata, for instance. Without the added tonal dimension of contrasting registration available on the organ much of the interlocking and sequential passage-work would lose its effect.

Having satisfied the twin calls of church and keyboard, and with only a short and hectic time in the orchestral environment of Cöthen, Bach afterwards turned to the trio format either to extend the potential of the keyboard as an obbligato instrument or on direct provocation from an eminent performer – Frederick the Great being the most eminent of them.

A number of other keyboard-orientated trios emerged,[3] prior to the royal command. Three featuring gamba (BWV 1027–1029) and the six with violin and obbligato keyboard (BWV 1014–1029) all pose problems of scoring. Two sources for the violin sonatas describe them as being 'à Cembalo [con]certato è Violino solo col Basso per Viola da Gamba accompagnata se piace . . .', a scoring which seems sensible in those passages where the harpsichord part

---

[1] Cf. the *Fifth Brandenburg Concerto* (the most *galant* example from that set) for the same combination of three soprano instruments, and also the sixth Concerto, which shows every sign of being an adaptation of a trio sonata.

[2] Cf. his extant instructions on registration, and the original scoring of the sinfonia mentioned above.

[3] The well-wrought, but harmonically unexciting trio sonata in C for two violins (BWV 1037, but now attributed to his pupil Goldberg) illustrates the increasingly lightweight use of the *allabreve stile antico* in chamber music from the 1720s onwards, which may still be observed in the fugal finales of early Mozart and Haydn string quartets.

consists of a figured bass alone, but requires discreet adaptation if a gamba is to play along with, for instance, the second and third movements of the A major sonata. Since the opening movement of BWV 1016 (E major) appears to be laid out for a pedal harpsichord (it is clearly an arrangement of some orchestral *sinfonia* similar to, e.g., the opening movement of Cantata 12), the gamba suggestion may be intended to apply when no pedal instrument is available. In any case, this style of movement has passed well beyond the concept of trio sonata writing.

In the gamba sonatas, the bass of the keyboard is frequently higher than the string line, and such crossings have led to the suggestion that a violone (at 16′ pitch) should be added to lower the real bass part by an octave. No bass player has ever been particularly attracted by this task, and it is more likely that the ear is expected (and in fact does) hear the gamba as if it were an octave higher than written (just as most recorder parts sound an octave lower than they really are).

The first of the three gamba sonatas, in G major, also offers problems of pedigree and precedence. One other complete version exists, scored for two flutes and continuo (BWV 1039), and the last movement also exists in a simplified version for organ (BWV 1027a). The differences of detail between the flute and gamba versions seem to indicate that the flute version came first. It is unlikely, for instance, that Ex. 25b overleaf would, on a reworking, have been altered to 25a. On the other hand, many of the adaptations of phrasing, although they may appear wayward to us, seem to encourage less uniformity between the voices than is demanded today (just as original fingerings in keyboard fugues actually encourage variants of phrasing for the subject).

The other two gamba sonatas, as also the violin and keyboard works, subscribe to a more *concertante* ideal. There is less true trio writing, more soloistic display (e.g. the two cadenza-like solos at the end of the D major gamba sonata), and a number of movements where the harpsichord part amounts to little more than an elaborated continuo accompaniment (e.g. the 'Erbame dich' Largo from the C minor violin sonata). The second version of the Adagio of Sonata 5 changed the arpeggiando accompaniment from semiquavers to demisemiquavers, and the sequence of remakes that the sixth violin sonata went through all increased the role of the keyboard – eventually one movement was annexed for *cembalo solo*.

Ex.25 Bach

(a) **Allegro ma non presto**

(b) **Allegro ma non tanto**

Interestingly, the movement that Bach finally omitted was a straight arrangement of the aria 'Heil und Segen' from Cantata 120, with the right hand of the harpsichord as the solo soprano.

A curious group of three sonatas, all related and all oddly 'charming' for J. S. Bach, demonstrate several stages of reworking. BWV 1038 (G major) is scored for flute, violin and continuo; in BWV 1022 (first published in 1936) the same music is transposed to F and given to obbligato harpsichord and *scordatura* violin (in this case tuned down a tone) – the change in tone quality is appealing, although there is no other occasion when Bach employs such a device. This oddity, and other 'modernisms' suggest that these trios may derive from some other member of the Bach household around 1730 (C. P. E. Bach?), although the pedigree of the bass line is indisputable. This is taken from a more recently discovered sonata for violin and basso continuo also in G major and certainly by J. S. Bach (BWV 1021), but with a quite different upper part added. It is in cases like this that we recall the descriptions of Bach's realisations left by his contemporaries:

Whoever wishes truly to observe what delicacy in thorough bass and very good accompanying mean need only take the trouble to hear our Kapellmeister Bach here, who accompanies every thorough bass to a solo so that one thinks it is a piece of concerted music and as if the melody he plays in the right hand were written beforehand. I can give a living testimony of this since I have heard it myself.[1]

Whatever the connection between the trio versions and J. S. Bach (and they may be the result of a teaching exercise), a comparison of the two G major versions indicates the potential for the inspired accompanist (Ex. 26).

Bach's second visit to the Court of Frederick the Great in Potsdam where Carl Philipp was employed as accompanist provoked the composition, hasty engraving and instant dispatch of the *Musicalisches Opfer* in the high hopes, one presumes, of some royal preferment that was never forthcoming. The dedication of this great set of ten canons, two *ricercare* and a trio sonata, all based on a theme suggested by the King, is dated a mere two months after the visit – 7 July 1747.[2] Two of the ensemble pieces have scoring indicated, no doubt with Frederick's flute playing in mind:

[1] Lorenz Mitzler, April 1738 (quoted in *The Bach Reader,* ed. David and Mendel).

[2] The agglomeration of 7s in the seventh month must have delighted Bach's numerological eye!

Ex.26   Bach

the valedictory *Canon Perpetuus* and the trio sonata, the largest of all the trios Bach produced, are both for flute, violin and continuo.[1] H. T. David's analysis of the *Musical Offering*[2] demonstrates that the symmetrical construction of the work as a whole required two complementary fugues in this central sonata. Bach's structure balances these elaborate masterpieces, where the King's Theme appears in the first as a *cantus firmus* and in the second as the actual fugue subject, translated into gigue rhythm, with two slow movements in the most modern *empfindsam* style. The sustained melodic interest of the Largo was produced from the essential devices of the *galant* manner – short, sighing phrases, drooping *appoggiature*, truncated arpeggio figuration – all held together over a gently pulsating bass. There is more *fiorature* in the Andante, and the same extremes of expressive nuance that Quantz recommended in his flute method. Although there is little else in Bach's output to match this style (except perhaps the 'Aus Liebe' aria from the *St Matthew Passion*, also for flute obbligato), Bach's eccentric skill at combining the best of both old and new sets him apart from both his country and his time.

Ex.27   Bach (*Musical Offering* Trio Sonata, mvt 3) realisation by [?] Kirnberger

[1] The realised continuo part for this trio attributed to Bach's pupil Kirnberger (reproduced in some modern editions) upsets many theories on the style and layout of mid-eighteenth-century harpsichord (or could it be fortepiano?) accompaniments.
[2] Schirmer (New York, 1945).

No royal preferment at least carried the compensation of no royal restrictions. Carl Philipp was sufficiently irked by Frederick's lack of interest in his music, but Quantz suffered still more from the King's proprietorial ban on any publication of his music. Only his flute method (see p. 119) spread his reputation abroad during his lifetime. Further west, Saxony had a 'protecteur des Muses' as possessive as Prussia's in King Friedrich August, to whom we must credit the total obscurity of Jan Dismas Zelenka. Only with the recent appearance of some of his church and orchestral music can we begin to take seriously one contemporary's claim that his keyboard music (now all lost) was as great as Bach's. A set of six 'Sonate à due Hautbois et Basson con due bassi obbligati' reinforces the recent reappraisal of Zelenka as a major musical architect. In sheer formal planning (with some fugue subjects more than twenty-five bars long), virtuoso demands on the two oboes, imaginative emancipation of the bassoon from the continuo bass line ('due bassi' include this divided bass) and a cheering touch of his native Bohemian folk music in each finale, these sonatas extend our view of the German repertoire and emphasise that nation's expertise in the use of woodwind.

Ex.28   Zelenka (Son. 1)

Variety of scoring became a hallmark of the North German composers from this period. According to Scheibe 'one sometimes takes flutes, oboes, violins or lutes alone; or two types of instrument, like a transverse flute and a violin, or an oboe and a bassoon; or else one may write for other instruments, combining them according to one's own choice'. Stöltzel (the composer of 'Bist du bei mir' copied by Bach into Anna Magdalena's notebook) suggested the obvious choice of violins/flutes/oboes for the top and bassoon/cello for the bottom parts, but Graupner and Fasch rose to such exotica as oboe d'amour, 'cornu du chasse',viola d'amore, chalumeau and even trumpet. Other nations at this time were determinedly antipathetic to wind instruments (excepting that gentleman's delight, the flute); Avison, like Burney, warned prospective users in England:

As to Wind-Instruments, these are all so different in their Tone, and in their Progressions through the various Keys, from those of the stringed Kind, besides the irremediable Disagreement of their rising in their Pitch, while the others are probably falling, that they should neither be continued too long in Use, nor employed but in such Pieces as are expressly adapted to them.[1]

Nevertheless, market requirements – and publishers now were looming large – decreed maximum flexibility, and the greatest success attended the most pragmatic composers. Telemann, the most 'modern' man in his sphere, acquired success without sacrificing his ideal: 'Whoever wants lifelong security must settle in a republic'. He had that enviable knack of writing music for which the player is grateful; he could accommodate the vulgar touch as well as the sophisticated nuance; he manipulated the new rococo gestures with more ease (though less depth) than Bach: journalist, publisher, linguist, lawyer – he was in fact everything to everyman (he even corresponded with Handel about botany).

Bach's surviving essays in trio sonata writing, small in extent though large in significance to the modern listener, were atypical. Telemann's vast output can be digested far more swiftly. As one of his pupils reported: 'He opened my eyes to music as a systematic art', adding nicely that he was not, however, 'Bach-correct'. Telemann's system implied facility without pedantry, but not inevitably the stereotype. In his most winning style he matched a felicitous sense of melody to an appropriateness of scoring which many a contemporary envied:

[1] *An Essay on Musical Expression* (London, 1752).

Ex.29   Telemann *(Essercizii Musici)*

The inventiveness of his music came partly from his easy absorption of current novelties: exotic tastes were put to work alongside didactic needs. The *3. methodische Trii* (for violins and flutes), for instance, offer ornamentation written-out to act as a model for the student (in which capacity they are still as relevant) while in the *Corellisirende Sonaten* he pays historical homage without parody.

Symptomatic of the widening frontiers of music and a testament to his value as an indicator of transition Telemann's feeling for the exotic went beyond the vulgar or the picturesque to assess the performances of alien styles with real sympathy. He worked for a while in what is now Poland, and found there new spices to add to the old brew. His own account of these field-trips, while staunchly maintaining the virtue of the Italian style to the bitter end, explains the engaging and enlivening mazurka-like music that suddenly appeared in his *Sonates polonoises*.

When the Court removed to Pless [Pszczyna] for six months, I heard there, as I had done in Cracow, the music of Poland and the Hanaka region of Moravia in

77

its true barbaric beauty. In the country inns the usual ensemble consisted of a violin tuned a third higher which could out-shriek half a dozen ordinary fiddles; a Polish bagpipe; and a regal. In respectable places, however, the regal was omitted and the number of fiddles and pipes increased; in fact I once heard thirty-six Polish pipes and eight Polish violins playing together. One would hardly believe the inventiveness with which these pipers and fiddlers improvise when the dancers pause for breath. An observer could collect enough ideas in eight days to last a lifetime. But enough; this music, if handled with understanding, contains much good material. In due course I wrote a number of grand concerti and trios which I clad in an Italian coat with alternating Allegri and Adagi.[1]

Ex.30 Telemann (*Sonate Polonoise*, no. 2)

---

[1] From Telemann's autobiography, included in Johann Mattheson, *Grundlage einer Ehrenpforte* (1740).

England

The arrival of Italian men, manners and music in England did not go without comment. The most diehard rejected out of hand the new fashions they brought with them. In *Musick's Monument* (1676) Mace decried the *'Scoulding Violins'* and lamented the days when music was performed

upon so many *Equal, and Truly-Sciz'd Viols*; and so *Exactly Strung, Tun'd, and Play'd upon*, as no one *Part* was any *Impediment* to the *Other* . . . *The Organ Evenly, Softly, and Sweetly Acchording to All* . . . But now the *Modes* and *Fashions* have cry'd *These Things* down, and set up a *Great Idol* in their Room; observe with what a *Wonderful Swiftness* They now run over their *Brave New Ayres*; and with what *High-Priz'd Noise, viz.* 10, or 20 *Violins*, &c., as I said before, to a *Some-Single-Soul'd Ayre*; which is rather fit to make a Mans *Ears Glow*, and fill his *Brains full of Frisks*, &c. than to *Season, and Sober his Mind, or Elevate his Affection* to *Goodness*.

But the more progressive had already been won over to the new instrument by the virtuosity of London players such as Davis Mell and John Banister, and were amazed by the new feats of the visitors. In 1659 Anthony à Wood reported: 'I saw Thomas Baltzar (the German violinist) run up his fingers to the end of the finger-board of the violin, and run them back insensibly, and all with great alacrity and very good time, which I nor any in England saw the like before.' English taste, which had at first dutifully followed the royal lead in preferring the French style – a legacy of Charles' 'travels' – now turned away from the *24 Violons* to the virtuosity of a single performer.

The arrival of the Italian virtuoso, Nicolai Matteis, brought matters to a head. 'He was an excellent musitian, and performed wonderfully upon the violin. His manner was singular . . . his *stoccatas, tremolos,* devisions, and indeed his whole manner was surprizing, and every stroke of his was a mouthfull. Beside, all that he played was of his owne composition. . . . I cannot but judge him to have bin second to Corelli', enthused North with that seasoning of mangled Italian that was to become the hallmark of the English amateur. Matteis' *Ayres for the Violin* were published in 1676: single pieces intended for solo violin, the composer himself selected 'from the movements here and there to make out admirable sonnatas'. Double-stopping was ingeniously indicated with notes outlined in dots for those who could manage it. Soon after, 'to oblige himself and to conforme to the English he made books of inner parts to those he had published, which brought in fresh ginnys', and the publication of a book of 'second trebles' two years later is an early indication of the new English taste for the trio sonata combination. But even in the revised version of these sonatas published in 1687, the predominance of the first violin betrays their solo origin:

Ex.31   Matteis

In fugal movements the distribution is, of necessity, less partial. As evidence of contemporary performance practice it is worth noting that the bass part contains figuring even when the 'Basso di Viola' alone is indicated without 'Cimbalo'. Purcell's sonatas contain similar ambiguities which strengthen the supposition that the figuring was a form of short score, rather than a playing indication (although e.g. Sonata III, 1683, refutes this).

There was every chance for the Italian style to take root in England so readily, since the ground had been well prepared for at least two generations. In the consort pieces of Gibbons, Lupo and Thomas Tomkins (see Ex. 1a, p. 7) three-part writing began to polarise towards SSB and the use of the organ 'acchording to all' in consort performance meant, in effect, a continuo part for much of the time. But, said the retrospective North in 1728, 'the old masters would not allow the liberty of playing from a thro-base figured, but they formed the organ part express because the holding out the sound required exact concord, else the consort would suffer; or perhaps the organists had not the skill as since, for now they desire only figures'. Treatises on figured-bass had been produced by William Penny, c.1670; Matthew Locke, in *Melothesia,* 1673; and by North himself, c.1710.

The 'old masters' included Ferrabosco and Coprario – 'who by the way was plain Cooper but affected an Itallian termination'. Their suites followed the French preference for dance sequences, but were scored for SSB and organ. John Jenkins, 'the mirrour of this our age', reflected most strongly the Italian violin style in the division writing for two 'trebles' (clearly violins) in his suites (Ex. 32). He was even mistakenly accredited with the production of the first set of trio sonatas in England, but the *12 Sonatas for 2 Violins and a Base with a Thorough Base for the Organ and Theorbo,* published c.1660 and mentioned by Hawkins (and, after him, Burney) have so far not materialised. Jenkins was certainly familiar with foreign sonata writing. The manuscript collection from the household of Francis North where he was employed included music by Colista, Cazzati, Stradella, Schmelzer and Degli Antonii – an exotic taste for the 1670s.[1] In his own suites Jenkins successfully blended the style of the 'fantasy suite' with the *concertante* element of Italy.

While Jenkins retired from London to the country to escape the effects of the Commonwealth, William Young found employment abroad in Austria. His three trio sonatas, published in Innsbruck in 1653 as part of an assorted collection of sonatas and dances for

[1] See p. 20.

Ex.32 Jenkins

2, 3 and 4 violins with continuo, therefore rank as the first 'English' examples of the form. All the separate 'Allemand, Correnti e Balletti' that make up the collection are also *à 3*, and may possibly have been intended to amplify the sonatas. These show so few effects of foreign virtuosity as to justify the adjective 'English': Young avoided dance movements (in title at least) and favoured the *canzona*, though curiously not as an internal movement in the manner of Purcell but almost always at the end. The harmonic daring so exploited in English fantasias reappears in these canzonas; a variety of 'points' is employed in the fast movements, and the second violin frequently lies higher than the first – a layout familiar from the masque music of William Lawes and Simon Ives.

We may suspect Young of bringing samples of continental sonata writing back to England in 1660, possibly supplying Francis North. He certainly influenced the style of Matthew Locke and his pupil, Purcell. The similarity between Young's sarabands and those that conclude Matthew Locke's suites is remarkable, and both are closely related to Purcell's *Largos* in 3/2. Of the three composers it was Locke who first attempted to standardise the movements of his suites, and regularise the sections of his *Consorts*. But he remained ambivalent about the use of a continuo instrument; the title-page of his *Little Consort* (for 'two trebles and a bass') says: 'To be performed either alone or with theorbo's and harpsechord'. There are obvious similarities also between Matthew Locke's Pavans, and the four (exercises?) by Purcell for the same scoring, in BM Add. 33236.

The twenty-two trio sonatas by Purcell stand in the same relationship to English music as Corelli's sonatas do to Italian. In the first place they are better than the products of his contemporaries. In the second they are the product of a felicitous synthesis, consolidating what still remained viable of the older consort idiom with the best features of the rival French and Italian manners. Purcell, almost alone of contemporaries, assessed the position of English music in the cross-winds of fashion with an objectivity surprising for one so involved.

Musick is but in its nonage; a forward child, which gives hope of what it may be hereafter in England, when the masters of it shall find more encouragement. 'Tis now learning Italian, which is its best master, and a little of the French air to give it somewhat more of gayety and fashion. Thus, being further from the sun we are of later growth than our neighbouring countries, and must be content to shake off our barbarity by degrees.

That was good fashionable talk in 1690; in the preface *To the Reader* from his *Sonnata's of III Parts* issued in 1683, he was less flattering about the French influence. Since it appears that this preface was, for once, the work of the composer rather than the publisher, it is worth quotation in full.

Instead of an elaborate harangue on the beauty and the charms of Musick (which after all the learned Encomions that words can contrive, commends it Self best by the performances of a skilful hand, and an angelical voice): I shall say but a very few things by way of Preface, concerning the following Book, and its Author: for its Author, he has faithfully endeavour'd a just imitation of the most fam'd Italian Masters; principally, to bring the Seriousness and gravity of that sort of Musick into vogue, and reputation among our Countrymen, whose humor, 'tis time now, should begin to loath the levity, and balladry of our neighbours: The attempt he confesses to be bold, and daring, there being Pens and Artists of more eminent abilities, much better qualify'd for the imployment than his, or himself, which he well hopes these his weak endeavours, will in due time provoke, and enflame to a more accurate undertaking. He is not asham'd to own his unskilfulness in the Italian Language; but that's the unhappiness of his Education, which cannot justly be accounted his fault, however he thinks he may warrantably affirm, that he is not mistaken in the power of the Italian Notes, or elegancy of their Compositions, which he would recommend to the English Artists. There has been neither care, nor industry wanting, as well in contriving, as revising the whole Work; which had been abroad in the world much sooner, but that he has now thought fit to cause the whole Thorough Bass to be Engraven, which was a thing quite besides his first Resolutions. It remains only that the English Practitioner be enform'd, that he will find a few terms of Art perhaps unusual to him, the chief of which are these following: *Adagio* and *Grave*, which import nothing but a very slow movement: *Presto Largo, Poco Largo,* or *Largo* by it self, a middle movement: *Allegro*, and *Vivace*, a very brisk, swift, or fast movement: *Piano*, soft. The Author has no more to add, but his hearty wishes, that his Book may fall into no other hands but theirs who carry Musical Souls about them; for he is willing to flatter himself into a belief, that with such his labours will seem neither unpleasant, nor unprofitable.

The importance of these instructions to the performer is patent, although it is worth emphasising that *Largo* indicates a moderate not a slow tempo. Purcell's praise of the 'most fam'd Italian Masters', good salemanship though it may be, seems excessive for one who only three years earlier had completed an exquisite set of (unpublished) consort *Fantazias* in compliment to the most homebred tradition. But the difference in style between fantazias and sonatas has been overstated. Despite his disavowal of the French levity, Purcell does include dance movements – minuets, sarabandes, gigues etc. – in the trios, although they are not so titled; and despite his omission of all mention of English influences in the preface, North could still write of this 'noble set of sonnatas, which however clog'd with somewhat of an English vein, for which they are unworthily despised, are very artificiall and good musick'.

The balance of influences has to be assessed with Purcell's market in mind. Clearly the pieces were aimed at those practitioners, like the Norths, who already favoured the Italian style, but were not equipped to decorate their adagios in the manner of Corelli; a more homophonic, harmonic style prevails, especially in the slow, non-dance movements. The French style, which Purcell was still employing so effectively in the theatre, provided no models for sonatas;[1] and since Grabu, the French Master of the King's Music, was discredited both politically and musically, there was everything to be gained by omitting references to France.

In short, there were no selling points for sonatas other than that they were Italianate. Another London advertisement by 'Mr August Keenall [Kühnel]' two years later for 'Several sonatas, composed after the Italian way' emphasises the point.

Only the publication of the first book of twelve *Sonnata's of III Parts: Two Viollins and Basse: To the Organ or Harpsecord* (1683) was supervised by Purcell; he even seems to have corrected misprints in his own hand. The second set of *Ten Sonata's in Four Parts* appeared two years after his death, in 1697, with a preface by his widow describing the works as 'having already found many Friends'. From this, and from their stylistically experimental nature we can deduce them to be earlier works than the 1683 set, probably put together from playing parts, although an autograph score does exist with six of them in fair copies by Purcell alongside the *Fantazias*.

Purcell organised the first eight sonatas of the 1683 set in pairs, one in the minor being followed by one in the relative major, and moving stepwise from flat to sharp keys. With Sonata No. 10 the sequence is broken, but significantly, the two sonatas that open the second set preserve the pattern of keys:

```
1683   g B♭   d F   a C   e G   c A   f D
1697                 [Son. 2] E♭ b [Son. 1]
```

In style these two sonatas are distinct from the 1697 set, and more similar to their predecessors; note particularly the repeated

[1] Save possibly for the 'Chacony' of the 1697 set.

dotted rhythms of their slow movements which hint at Matthew Locke more strongly than at any foreigner:

Ex.33   Purcell (Son. I, 1697)

Much effort has been spent to discover Italian imitation in both sets of sonatas. Colista's music was certainly known to Purcell, who quoted an example of fugue from one of Colista's sonatas in 1683. Sonatas by Cazzati,[1] Vitali and Bassani were available in England, and the travels of Matteis and Young must have supplied many more manuscript examples. Corelli's Op. 1, now known to have been published in 1681 rather than 1683, is another attractive candidate. But rather than dissection in the light of Purcell's sales

[1] A sheet of Cazzati's sonatas Op. 18 (nos. 11 & 12) was used as a wrapper for the score of Purcell's *Birthday Ode* of 1690 (Bodley MS Mus.C.26).

talk, these incomparable pieces would be better served by the publication of playing parts for the modern performer; no complete set of string parts has been in print since the seventeenth century.

Of the two sets, the 1683 certainly received the finer publication; the part-books were beautifully engraved by Cross and carefully corrected. The second collection, inelegantly printed from moveable type, may have been cheaper for Mrs Purcell but presents many more difficulties for the player, particularly the haphazard jumble of figures in the continuo part. From Playford's advertisements we know that Purcell intended the bass string part for bass viol rather than bass violin, but the choice of keyboard instrument seems to have been left open. Thurston Dart pointed out the probability that the sparse figuring in the thorough-bass part suggested the sustained and simple harmonies of the organ. On the other hand North in 1698 remarked on 'the Monopoly of the Harpsichord in consort, excluding all other touch instruments and even the Organ itself' and reported that his brother 'caused the devine Purcell to bring his Itallian manner'd compositions; and with him on his harpsicord, my self and another violin, wee performed them more than once'.

Purcell's apologies in his preface show that he first intended to publish the *Twelve Sonatas* in three part-books, leaving the keyboard player to simplify and harmonise the bass line in the traditional way. Prompted by the arrival of new publications from Amsterdam and Italy, he decided to produce the separate part for keyboard: presumably Playford, his publisher, was not prepared to re-engrave the title-page, and hence the discrepancy in titling between the first and second sets. All Purcell's trio sonatas contain movements in dance-metre, although being ostensibly *da chiesa*; they may even have been performed, with amplified forces, in the Chapel Royal, where the dance movements would have delighted their royal dedicatee. The sarabandes in particular have the air of theatre tunes, and often the rhythmic flexibility of a French chaconne, while the canzonas and gigues call to mind the English song and dance idiom (Ex. 34a overleaf). Only occasionally did Purcell employ a head theme with really Italian connotations, such as the canzona subject 'in tromba' from the D major sonata of 1697 (Ex. 34b), or the subject of Sonata I (1683), which is almost identical with one of Bassani's canzona openings (Ex. 34c):

Ex.34

(a) Purcell (Son. X, 1697)

(b) Purcell (Son. I, 1683)

(c) Bassani (Op. 5 no. 7)

The attractive idea of a coda, or *petite reprise,* played *piano* (Sonatas II and X (1683) and VII and IX (1697)) came from North Italy; the English preferred the slow or 'drag' codas of Jenkins and Locke (Sonata III, 1697).

Technical ingenuities abound, but are rarely spotlit. The 'Canon by two-fold augmentation in the 5th and 8th above' (Sonata VI, 1683) stems from the canonic devices of such composers as Buonamente, but is more immediately related to the technical instruction that Purcell had contributed to Playford's *Introduction to the Skill of Musick* in the same year. The great 'Chacony' in G minor (Sonata VI, 1697), constructed over an unchanging 5-bar ground, is the longest single movement in Purcell's chamber music. It mixes canonic and rhythmic complexities with the same juxta-position of French and Italian styles that Couperin later employed in *L'Amphibie.* The curious key order of the 1697 sonatas, where the 'Chacony' is the second of two G minor sonatas, suggests that they may have been intended for performance in sequence; a chaconne often ended a collection (as in Vivaldi and Corelli), and Frances Purcell's ordering of these works was probably not that envisaged by her husband.

Only the ninth sonata of the second set achieved popularity in the eighteenth century; it was republished in 1704 as 'That Excellent Sonata in F . . . call'd The Golden Sonata' – the first time the nickname was applied. Since descriptive titles of commendation were never used at this time, one looks for some musical source for the adjective. Given the cavalier attitude of the English to foreign words, two possible but tentative candidates might be Bertali's Sonata *Taussent Gulden* (see Ex. 19, p. 57) or Vitali's *La Guidoni* of 1669. Both are in F major, with the triadic patterning of the *Golden Sonata* in their basic themes; Vitali's sonata bears resemblances not only in themes, but in its distribution of slow movements, and its repeated-note harmonic sequences. In Purcell's possible derivative we have an example of the composer's reconsideration of the use of the Italian homophonic *adagio* to punctuate or link movements. The autograph, a fair copy, has a correction slip pasted over the end of the *canzona* of the Golden Sonata which revises the original adagio ending to what we now know (Ex. 35). Possibly this was to avoid killing the effect of the *grave* that followed; in any case it demonstrates Purcell's concern for the overall patterning of his sonatas, and the coherence of adjacent movements.

One ingenious example of modern reconstruction, which adds one trio sonata to the canon of twenty-two, should be mentioned here. Thurston Dart pointed out that the so-called 'Violin Sonata in G minor' is in fact a trio sonata for the typical North European combination of violin, bass viol and organ. The simplified bass part, and the absence of imitative entries in the canzona and final gigue led him to supply the missing bass viol part and bring the work into line with similar pieces by e.g. Becker, who published *Sonatas for a violin, Viol da Gamba and Basso continuo* in 1668. Burney remarked that they 'were well known during the latter end of the last century', which adds weight to Dart's supposition.

By the turn of the century the circulation of Corelli's sonatas had, according to North, 'cleared the ground of all other sorts of musick whatsoever'. Purcell's works were surprisingly little imitated, but at least one Englishman turned his attention to the Italian style so successfully that his sonatas were for a long time published as Corelli's – Ravencroft's Op. 1 circulated as Corelli's Op. 7 by the deception of the Parisian publisher Le Cène. They are well worth attention as being (to quote Alfred Einstein) 'more like Corelli's than Corelli's own sonatas'. William Corbett (secret agent

Ex.35   Purcell (Son. IX, 1697)

First Version   **Adagio**

and composer) supplied trios for the 'flute' (i.e. the recorder),
which indicate the English popularity of that instrument as do the
transpositions of Corelli's sonatas published by Walsh and the
publications by Robert Valentine and William Williams (including
the latter's attractive 'Sonata in imitation of Birds'). Contrapuntal
movements gave the greatest problems to all imitators; a Corellian
grave was not difficult, depending as it did on spontaneous embellishment by the performers. But 'the great danger in conducting
fugues is the going too farr for variety and so by tossing the point
from key to key the ayre of the genuine key is lost' said North.
James Sherard, a London chemist, was one who attempted the style
(Opp. 1 and 2), but the result was judged 'dull and overdriven'.
Four (unpublished) trios by William Croft are the most assured

products of the new century's first decade; three (E minor, B minor, Bb major) draw largely on Corelli (with *prestissimo* running basses), but the trio in F major appears to be a gloss, movement by movement, on Purcell's *Golden Sonata*.

By 1712 the English had a new master in the invention of 'ayre' and the expansive use of harmony. For more than half a century the shadow of Handel lay over the trio sonata output of this country. Only Arne, Boyce and Geminiani possessed the individuality to escape the blanket apology of 'Handelian'.

Handel was never primarily a purveyor of instrumental music; he was a man of the theatre and later, by derivation, of the oratorio world. The trio sonatas reflect his immersion in this theatrical milieu almost as much as they hark back to his pre-English career. What, for instance, could be more operatic than the opening bars of the Largo in the first of the Op. 2 sonatas (Ex. 36)?

Predictably enough, the idea stems originally from Keiser's opera *Octavia*, and then recurs in a modified form as 'Comfort ye' in *Messiah*. As with many of Handel's 'germ' themes, the instrumental version seems to be a stepping stone *en route* to some grander transformation, and so betrays little concern with specific instrumental colouring.

A set of early trios for two oboes and bassoon cannot seriously be considered as genuine; when shown them, Handel merely remarked 'I used to write like the devil in those days, but chiefly for the hautbois' – a fair disclaimer for works he failed to recognise. His Op. 2 trios[1] with their optional scoring for 'two violins, flutes or hoboys' were designed to appeal to the growing number of wind players in London. Opus 5 was published six years later in 1738; more than 30 of its 40 movements consist of arrangements of movements from other larger-scale pieces (*Terpsicore*, *Athalia*, *Alcina* etc.) which may well have been assembled by the astute Walsh rather than by the composer himself. The viola part in No. 4 was not in fact intended for the trio set and comes from the original orchestral version of this material. Trio sonatas were a commercial venture rather than a musical necessity for Handel, and this attitude is reflected in both their fabric and their form.

The distinction between 'aria' and 'instrumental' types of trio writing is far less apparent in Handel than in Bach. Handel fre-

[1] Originally 6 sonatas: Nos. 7–9 were added by Chrysander in the *Handel Gessellschaft*.

Ex.36 Handel (Op. 1 no. 1)

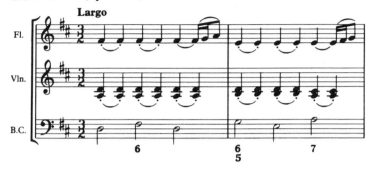

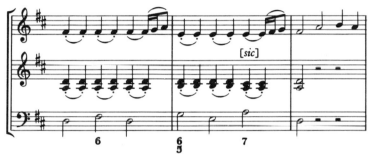

quently tried to make his chamber music live up to the techniques and expectations of theatrical creations, by a distribution of parts derived from the vocal duet rather than the solo aria with obbligato. There is an immediate air of opera about the way a lyrical solo line is divided up between the two protagonists with no loss of continuity and a great gain in spatial drama:

Ex.37   Handel (Op. 2 no. 8)

The fugal movements of the trios, surprisingly enough, show Handel at his least exciting. While the subjects are invariably arresting (such as the syncopated theme from Op. 2 no 9, which Romain Rolland claims to be an English folk tune), episodic treatment interrupts the contrapuntal discussion, and the contrived modulations that North deplored are too much in evidence.

The concertante sections of such pieces as Op. 2 nos. 4 and 9 call for the virtuoso player; and while such favourite sonatas as Op. 2 no. 8 clearly need two violins, no. 5 is ideal for a combination of traverso and violin. No. 4 may well have been written for the popular English combination of two flutes. Two separate sonatas for wind show Handel using his favourite germ themes. The sonata for two traversi in E minor, probably written during his stay at Canons between 1718 and 1720, ends with a movement based on the theme of the Oboe Concerto No. 3 (Finale) and the Organ Concerto Op. 4 no. 3/ii. More intriguingly, an unpublished sonata for two recorders (its component parts now split between England and America) demonstrates an otherwise unknown extension of the familiar 12/8 theme from the recorder sonata/organ concerto, Op. 1 no. 11/Op. 4 no. 5.

Ex.38 Handel

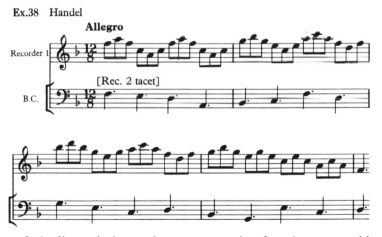

It is disappointing to have no example of a trio sonata with obbligato keyboard from the eighteenth century's greatest all-round performer on 'touch instruments', but the C major sonata with gamba (H.G. vol. 48) attributed to Handel is actually by the Dutch composer Leffloth. Its third movement, however, is of interest, as a fully written out example of *arpeggiando* accompaniment.

Geminiani was an even more assiduous re-writer than Handel: a characteristic which hardly agrees with Tartini's description of him as 'Il Furibundo'. His solo violin sonatas, for which he was most noted, were put through various transformations which reflect both the taste and performing practice of the times; six of his Op. 1 solo sonatas reappeared in trio form (following the technique of Matteis?) published by Walsh *c.*1740. Geminiani's addition of the second part reveals the three-part thinking implicit in many eighteenth-century themes – although no continuo player would have been expected to make the third part explicit. A comparison of the solo Sonata No. 1 with its trio version demonstrates that the continuation of the first violin theme is actually a countersubject to the unwritten point of imitation (Ex. 39).

The three sonatas constructed from Scotch airs which appear in Geminiani's invaluable *Treatise of Good Taste in the Art of Musick* indicate the direction of public taste in the 1740s towards *galanterie*.

Amongst native composers, some of the older styles of trio writing were reinstated by William Boyce, much to the approval of the public and Charles Burney:

His next publication was *Twelve Sonatas or Trios for Two Violins and a Base*, which were longer and more generally purchased,[1] and performed, and admired, than any productions of the kind in this kingdom except those of Corelli. They were not only in constant use, as chamber Music, in private concerts, for which they were originally designed, but in our theatres, as act-tunes, and public gardens, as favourite pieces, during many years.

Boyce's royal appointment to a Handelian monarch (and his deafness) curbed his experiments with the lighter fashions and we find once more a true antiphonal use of the two violins combined with the 'classic' poise of unhurried fugal writing. Counterpoint predominates in the odd-numbered sonatas, all of which contain at least one fugue; a strict canon at the fifth and the octave is included in Sonata No. 9. Boyce's strength lies as much in his variety as his melodic appeal, however. No two sonatas follow the same scheme; sturdy gavottes and minuets contrast with 'affetuoso' and 'gratioso' melodies: Sonata No. 6 includes a Corellian *allemanda*, while the middle movement of No. 4 is a slow March.

The rather less varied set of seven trio sonatas by Arne (a curiously random number for an eighteenth-century publication)

---

[1] With nearly 600 subscribers (including Pepusch, Handel and Arne) this publication was exceptionally successful in eighteenth-century terms.

Ex.39   Geminiani (Op. 1 no. 10)

are rescued by the composer's 'God-gifted genius for melody', a virtue granted to him even by Stafford Smith who nevertheless found him 'a conceited Papist, and an evil living man'. As a Catholic he had no Court commitments, and as a melodist little interest in polyphony; only the occasional (unintended?) melodic similarities give his sets of movements any unity. Like Handel, Arne appears to have needed a text to excite his best ideas.

Six trios by Gluck, published during his only visit to London in 1746, are written in the three-movement form of Sammartini:

slow-fast-fast. The strict, though not inspired, canon that ends the first sonata does give the lie to Handel's remark that his cook knew more counterpoint than Gluck!

A list of names serves to identify the forces that so effectively invaded the English scene between 1710 and 1755, drawn on by rumour of the ease with which the public would 'drop their pence' for music: Lampugnani, Zuccari, Pasquali (author of the treatise on continuo accompaniment), Galeotti and Cirri were all primarily Italian *players*. Their occasional trio publications are mentioned by Newman, together with the revealing statistic that while there were three Italian sonata writers in England prior to 1710, there were sixteen active during the next half-century. Roger North's encouragements had come home with a vengeance.

France

The imperial confidence of France, and its centralisation on Paris, protected that country from Italian invasion for longer than any other stronghold in Europe. The model for musical activities was set by the Court at Versailles, where taste had been moulded by the dictatorship of Lully and did *not* condone sonatas. Even as late as 1732 the Abbé Pluche could decry such works as the musical equivalent of spotty paper in painting, and Fontenelle could voice his annoying flippancy: 'Sonate, que me veux-tu?'[1] By then most of Europe would have sided with the Italophile Burney: 'the Sonata should answer: "I would have you listen with attention and delight to the ingenuity of the composition, the neatness of the execution, sweetness of the melody, and the richness of the harmony, as well as to the charms of refined tones, lengthened and polished into passion"'.

In the early eighteenth century the battle of styles intensified as the French fought a desperate rearguard action against the steadily encroaching Italians. French propaganda, fast, furious and verbose as it was, did not aim at something so incidental as chamber music; its first target was the opera and its second the exaggerations to which Italians were prone. Raguenet, more balanced than most of his contemporaries (Le Cerf, for example, or Le Blanc) gave this description of a solo performer, based on hearsay about Corelli's playing:

The *French* in their Airs aim at the Soft, the Easie, the Flowing, and Coherent. . . . The *Italians* venture at ev'ry thing that is harsh, and out of the way, but then they do it like People that have a right to venture, and are sure of Success. . . . As the *Italians* are naturally much more brisk than the *French*, so are they more sensible of the Passions, and consequently express 'em more lively in all their Productions. If a Storm, or Rage, is to be describ'd in a Symphony, their Notes gives us so natural an Idea of it, that our Souls can hardly receive a stronger Impression from the Reality than they do from the Description; every thing is so brisk and piercing, so impetuous and affecting, that the Imagination, the Senses, the Soul, and the Body it self are all betray'd into a general Transport; 'tis impossible not to be born down with the Rapidity of these Movements: A Symphony of Furies shakes the Soul; it undermines and overthrows it in spite of all its Care; the Artist himself, while he is performing it, is seiz'd with an unavoidable Agony, he tortures his Violin, he racks his Body; he is no longer Master of himself, but is agitated like one possest with an irresistable Motion.

[1] But where, when and to whom?

His account of the different techniques in scoring for two violins is lucid and dispassionate:

But if we now proceed from the simple Airs to a Consideration of those Pieces that consist of several Parts, we there shall find the mighty Advantages the *Italians* have over the *French*. I never met with a Master in *France*, but what agreed, that the *Italians* knew much better how to turn, and vary a *Trio* than the *French*. Among us the first upper Part is generally beautiful enough; but then the second usually descends too low to deserve our Attention. In *Italy* the upper Parts are generally three or four Notes higher than in France; so that their Seconds are high enough to have as much Beauty as the very First with us.[1]

With less moderation Le Cerf retaliated:

The first trebles of the Italians squeak because they are too high. Their second trebles have the fault of being too close to the first, and too far from the bass, which is the third part. These are two disagreements. I find it advantageous and profitable to make the second treble into a tenor, as we do – and not another treble as do the Italians – because the tenor occupies the distance between the bass and the treble and thus binds the chords of the trio. Instead, when the second treble is so high, it leaves too much of an interval and space between the first treble and the bass. So that it is not our fault that the second parts of our trios are only tenors. On the contrary, I maintain that the body of the trio is better off for it.

Examples of the less 'squeaky' instrumentation he may have had in mind include the *Pièces en Trio* of Marin Marais (1692) 'Pour les Flutes, Violon & Dessus de Viole' with continuo. This scoring was a speciality of northern Europe (we have met it in works by Ferrabosco, Coprario, Purcell and Buxtehude, for example), but the particular cultivation of the *basse de viole* was a feature of the French court. Marais' music was reported by Walther to be known all over Europe, a rare achievement for a Frenchman (and one that should be repeated today). His exquisite set of *Pièces à une et à deux Violes* from 1686 provide the unusual sonority of trio scoring for two *bass* instruments, and show how little Marais was indebted to cisalpine influence. The *Tombeau de Mr. Meliton,* for instance, with its harmonic profundity and multiple stopping for the viols, derives from the style of the lutenists rather than the string players:[2]

---

[1] *A Comparison Between the French and Italian Musick,* Paris 1702, transl. Galliard (?), London 1709.

[2] It must surely have been commercial aspiration that led Marais to suggest the alternatives of 'organ, harpsichord, violin, treble viol, theorbo, guitar, transverse flute, recorder or oboe' in Book III of the *Pièces de Viole* (1711).

Ex.40 Marais

It was about this time, according to Couperin, that the first
Italian sonatas were heard in France; Corrette substantiates this

with a claim that at a concert given by the Abbé Mathieu the 'trios of Corelli, printed in Rome appeared for the first time. This new kind of music encouraged all composers to work in a more brilliant style. . . .' But Couperin's half-serious account of his own ventures into this sphere imply that, while Italian music might be admired, no French prophet would be accepted in his own country. In 1726, when he published his trios as *Les Nations*, he revealed the tale of their first appearances:

It has already been several years since some of these trios were composed. Several of those manuscripts have circulated, which I mistrust because of the negligence of copyists. From time to time I have added to their number, and I believe that the lovers of true music will be pleased with them. The first sonata in this collection was also the first that I composed and the first that was composed in France. The story of it is curious in itself.

Charmed by those [sonatas] of Signor Corelli, whose works I shall love as long as I live, much as [I shall love] the French works of Monsieur de Lulli, I attempted to compose one, which I had performed in the hall where I had heard those of Corelli. Knowing the greediness of the French for foreign novelties above all else, and lacking confidence in myself, I did myself a very neat service by means of a convenient little ruse. I pretended that a relative of mine – in the service of the King of Sardinia, to be exact – had sent me a sonata by a new Italian composer. I rearranged the letters of my name so that it became an Italian name,[3] which I used instead. The sonata was devoured eagerly and I felt vindicated by it. Meanwhile, that gave me courage. I wrote others; and my Italianized name brought much applause to me, under the disguise. Fortunately, my sonatas won enough favour that the deception did not embarrass me at all. I have compared these sonatas with those that I wrote since, and have neither changed nor added much of importance. I have only added some big suites of pieces to which the sonatas serve merely as preludes or kinds of introductions.

Prior to this publication Couperin had written a total of four sonatas. In *Les Nations* he changed the titles of three of them, omitted one (*La Steinquerque*, named after the French victory of 1692) and included a new sonata, called grandly *L'Impériale*. By adding dance suites to the sonatas he built a compound form which further south would have been called a *sonata da camera* but which Couperin entitled an 'ordre'. We have no precise date for the original four sonatas, but the derivation of the final publication looks something like this:

*c.*1692	*Les Nations* (1726)
La Pucelle	→ Ordre 1. La Françoise (+ 8 dances)

[1] 'Pernucio' and 'Coperuni' are two possible anagrams.

La Visionnaire	→ Ordre 2. L'Espagnole (+ 10 dances)
	Ordre 3. L'Impériale (+ 9 dances)
L'Astrée	→ Ordre 4. La Piémontoise (+6 dances)
La Steinquerque	(not published)

Couperin had already offered in *Les Goûts Réünis* (1724) a manifesto of his supra-national feelings:

The Italian and French styles have for a long time shared the Republic of Music in France. For my part, I have always esteemed works that seemed to merit admiration without regard for either author or nation; and the first Italian sonatas which appeared in Paris more than thirty years ago, and which encouraged me to compose some myself, to my mind wronged neither the works of M. de Lully, nor those of my ancestors, who will always be more admirable than imitable. And so by right of my neutrality, I remain under the benevolent influences that have guided me until now.

By patriotically subtitling his new collection *Sonades et Suite de Simphonies en Trio* (he never used the Italian 'sonata'), Couperin laid emphasis on his absorption of the best aspects of Corelli's style. *La Pucelle*, for example, opens with the descending chromatic line that also occurs in the Grave of *L'Astrée* – more an operatic touch than a crib from Corelli – Ex. 41, overleaf.

Although he allowed a *tremolo* effect in the *Légèrement* of *La Pucelle,* Couperin restrained his violins from wild leaps and cross-string writing; all the passage-work in the two gigue-like sections moves scalewise. The charming *Air* which precedes the final *Gigue* (a feature of three of the sonatas) is a perfectly French *brunette* melody divided between the two violins in alternation with hardly more than a couple of bars of trio writing. In the dance movements of *Les Nations* that follow these *Sonades* one senses an alignment rather than a reconciliation of opposing tastes.

The *Grande Sonade en Trio* added at the end of the ten *Concerts* announced a true détente between the two styles in its very title: *Le Parnasse, ou L'Apothéose de Corelli*. Even more successfully than *L'Apothéose de Lulli*, which was published the following year, this sonata supplies the answer to what Couperin actually meant by a 'reunion' of the styles. In the later sonata the programmatic meeting of Lully and Corelli decrees a certain artificiality to those sections which (in the most subtle way) parody the rival styles of violin playing. The imitation of the 'trembleurs' scene from Lully's *Isis* for the *Rumeur souteraine* is an effective pun, but since both styles cannot sit equally happily over the Corellian walking-bass, the bass

Ex.41   Couperin

becomes of necessity more involved in the musical argument. And even with the plot to assist them sixteen individual movements, in six different keys, adhere uneasily.

L'Apothéose de Corelli precipitates a true synthesis in its opening bars, where a really Corellian violin line, set over an impeccable andante bass, is graced in the French style. The transition into the

Italian sequential spiral at bars 5–8 is covered by a suspension so typical of the French that the deception passes notice. The wide Italianate leaps in the fugue, when Corelli 'marque sa joye', are tempered by a 'tremblement appuyé' introduced into the first bar of the subject. The whole sonata is filled with subtleties of this nature, from the 'notes égales' that flow as Corelli drinks at the fount of inspiration to the sudden *tirades* that indicate his 'entousiazme' and the almost totally off-beat subject of the final fugue. Couperin made an inspired amalgamation of the strengths of the rival styles. To quote Motteux on Purcell, faced with a similar dilemma some thirty years earlier, he 'joins to the delicacy and beauty of the Italian way the graces and gaiety of the French'.

Couperin scored the upper parts of the trios for *premier dessus* and *deuxième dessus*; violins are the obvious choice, although in the *Plaintes* of the 'Lully' sonata he suggested flutes, or violins 'très adoucis'. In an *Avis* he also noted the expedient of playing the trio on two harpsichords, each performer playing the bass line and one of the upper parts, when it was impossible to assemble 'quatre personnes, faisant leur profession de la Musique'.[1] This instrumentation would at least solve the problem of a low F$\sharp$ in the last movement of the 'Lully' sonata – below the range even of the violin.

In his conscious acknowledgement of the twin sources of his art, Couperin recognised the limitations of Lully's legacy in non-dramatic contexts – hence, one suspects, the conscientious titling of the *Apothéoses*. Both in France and abroad the 'French influence' in sonata writing was a theatrical manner applied to chamber music, whereas the Italian was the more direct effect of sonata on sonata.

Among Couperin's contemporaries, Jean-Fery Rebel was singled out by the partisan Le Cerf for special mention: 'Rebel has indeed caught some of the flare and fire of the Italians; but he has had the good taste and sense to temper these with the gentleness and wisdom of the French, and he has abstained from those frightening and monstrous cadenzas that are the delight of Italians'. Rebel's saving in Le Cerf's eyes was a partiality for French dance forms: he was most successful with his choreographic *simphonies*, which were written for performance by the leading dancers of the *Opéra*.

[1] Is this the only reference to *professional* performance of published trios?

His debt to Lully, who taught him composition, can be seen in the *Douze sonates à II et III parties* (1712–13) with their sequence of dance movements headed by literary titles, and in the *12 Sonates à violon seul mellées de plusieurs récits pour la Viole*. In these, as in several of Couperin's *Concerts Royaux*, the 'récits' frequently convert the texture to three independent parts.

Sébastien de Brossard, who has already been quoted for his dictionary definition of sonata forms (p. 16), stands out as an enlightened antiquarian. His library included a large volume of string sonatas by Austrian and Italian composers, bought from the Strasbourg estate of François Rost in 1698. This neglected collection[1] with over 120 trio sonatas (Cazzati, Vitali, Bertali, Schmelzer, Rosenmüller are among the named composers), provided the material for his definition, and enlarges our picture of foreign music available to the French prior to 1700. In his *Catalogue* Brossard admitted that 'All the composers of Paris, above all the Organists, had at that time [1695] a fever, as it were, to compose *Sonates à la manière Italienne*', and it seems that French capitulation to the Italian forms was as sudden as it had been delayed. By 1713 a writer in Paris could report that 'Cantatas and sonatas spring right out of the ground here; no musician arrives without a sonata or cantata in his pocket; there isn't a soul who doesn't want to compose his own set to be engraved and so outsmart the Italians on their own ground'. Only those composers who were, or had been, connected with the royal establishment and the *24 Violons,* had a vested interest in the Lullian style and resisted the advances of the Corellians. These Italianate forces were led by Mascitti, a pupil of the master, and later by Jean-Marie Leclair, described by Blainville as 'the Corelli of France'.

One result of the Italian invasion was an emphasis on the solo sonata, a better vehicle for virtuosity than the trio. An offshoot of this, anticipated by Elizabeth Jacquet de la Guerre, was the keyboard sonata 'with violin accompaniment', a form which provides the bridge between rococo and classical chamber music. However, despite the 'fever to compose sonatas in the Italian style', few masterpieces emerged. Mascitti's few trios repeated the mannerisms of Corelli without their poise, and Dornel's accommodating *Suittes en trio pour les flûtes, violons, hautbois* (1709) only become effective when scored up for orchestral use – an 'improvement' essential to

[1] Now in the Bibliothèque Nationale (Rés. Vm^7 673).

a lot of French music published in reduced form.

Leclair, therefore, stands out for more reason than just having been murdered one night – reputedly on his wife's instructions. His solo writing (particularly 'Le Tombeau' sonata) is still favoured by modern players for its virtuosity, and his advances in double-stopping were noted with approval in 1738. The *Mercure* claimed that he had 'pushed this device so far that even the Italians themselves confessed that he was a master of the style' – slightly ambiguous grounds for flattery! On his own evidence, however, Leclair was not seeking to impress by technical means. Like Couperin, he asked for restraint in adding embellishments to his written lines ('which serve only to disfigure them') a failing to which the Italians were prone. In the *Ouvertures et Sonates en trio* (Op. 13, 1753) he insisted that movements marked 'allegro' were not to be played too fast: 'those who push the tempo too much, above all in the serious pieces such as the Fugues in 4/4, merely trivialise the melody'. The 'trio' component of Op. 13 contains transcriptions of three solo sonatas from an earlier collection, with added second violin parts in the manner of Geminiani, and a scored-down trio arrangement of the overture to *Scylla et Glaucus*. But the six sonatas of Op. 4 (*c*.1730) are real trios, which may even be performed on two viols as an alternative to violins. Leclair's treatment of slow movements in particular indicates his freedom within the Corellian mould; the *Siciliano* of Sonata No. 2 contains a degree of counterpoint unusual for either French or Italians, worked with the harmonic sophistication of a Bach or Handel. Again unlike his contemporaries, Leclair maintained a feeling for the long cantabile line, at a period when rococo fragmentation was more and more in vogue.

Ex.42   Leclair (Op. 4 no. 2)

On the other hand, Leclair softened the sharp edge of Teutonic contrapuntal writing by burying his main themes in a 'thickening' of extra counterpoint. Instead of making a fresh entry with the subject in a fugue, an individual part will proceed without a break from passage-work to theme and back again. In Op. 4 no. 2, for example, the countersubject of the fugue anticipates the entry of the subject proper; and in the final movement the second violin quotes the fugal theme shorn of its opening note. The *style galant,* to which such movements lean, was always more concerned with sonorities than thematic working-out.

The only other French trios comparable with Leclair's are the Op. 2 set by Mondonville (1734), each featuring a double-fugue ending in a pedal-point (a curiously un-French device). Despite the suggestion of violins or flutes, the frequent double-stopping and the wide range of the Allegros insist on violins. They are almost the last of the French trios to give fair shares to each player including the cello. Mondonville later explored more modern territories of obbligato harpsichord writing, and the accompanied keyboard sonata, both forms that were about to receive international approval as vehicles for the new 'style galant'.

The outcome of more than fifty years of industry by the French to produce a Gallic synthesis of the national styles was, in fact, the creation of an international vernacular for music, which, though carrying a French title, could dispense with all national frontiers.

Rococo

One cannot, unless by reversion to a Darwinian ideal of musical progress, speak of the death of a form or the decline of a technique. No form can, of itself, be unfit for its content, any more than an instrument *per se* can be described as 'degenerate' – nowadays a favourite adjective for the late-eighteenth-century harpsichord. *Style* is the mortal component, and, as in contemporary *haute couture*, the more widespread its acceptance, the more frequent the obligation to change. The landscape of music is barren only in those rare conditions when the natural tensions between style and form are artificially constrained, and a static, petrified state is demanded. The more compliant artists of Frederick the Great's court were typical victims of this braking process.

When J. S. Bach advertised his *Clavier Übung* in 1731 as containing *Galanterien*, his intention was not to kill the old nationalistic styles, but unwittingly he accelerated the infection of the whole of Europe with its first truly international style for more than a century and a half. The 'homme galant' was an up-to-date dilettante in the best sense of the word. Nothing could have been more appropriately hybrid than the 'galant' style: a French adjective celebrating the acceptance of Italian fluency first circulated by Germans. 'Noble simplicity' was a slogan accepted by the élite of every nation – for the moment – and philosophers sprang forward to explain its application to music: 'If music is to move us, to please us, to keep our interest and our attention, it must sing,' wrote Rousseau in 1764. He continued:

I therefore conclude that all music that doesn't sing is tiresome no matter what its harmony. Melodic unity demands that we never hear two tunes at once, though this does not mean that the tune must always be in the same part, indeed the handling of the transition of the tune from one part to another, even from the vocal line to the accompaniment, this is something in which there are plenty of opportunities for displaying elegance and taste. I conclude that all music in which several tunes are going on at once is bad music, and that the result is the same as when two or three people talk at once at the same pitch. Music, like painting, must remind us of natural truth.

The trio sonata was clearly far from revealing the 'natural truth'. This could be rectified, of course, by encouraging that imbalance in part-writing which had already been practised by the melodists. What is there to suggest, for instance, that this familiar tune had anything to do with the trio sonata concept?

Ex.43 Pergolesi [attrib.] (Son. 1)

Pergolesi's treatment of that theme (and Stravinsky's afterwards) presupposes that it is a unit of melody, best displayed against an anonymous background: used for what it is, not for what it might imply. For a composer who died in 1736, the style – and even the title – of the *Twelve Sonatas for Two Violins and a Bass or an Orchestra* is prophetic. We may well side with Burney and doubt the attribution to Pergolesi, for as examples of the 'melody with accompaniment' trio these pieces typify the 1770s when they were actually published.[1] Leclair and Geminiani had foreshadowed the domination by the first violin by rewriting their 'solo' sonatas as trios; this emphasis took over almost completely during the period from Sammartini to Boccherini – and even to Haydn.

It is more difficult to pinpoint the end of a style than its beginning – an overhang of the old idiom, an unwitting prophecy of the new, or the over-enthusiasm which attends any novelty can

[1] Domenico Gallo is the more probable author (see RISM).

so easily distort the picture. In this particular no-man's-land of music, the rarity of modern performances makes it even more difficult to evaluate developments within, for instance, the 'singing-allegro' or the 'galant-andante' of the mid-eighteenth century.

Musical styles do not change with the rapidity of chemical reactions; the melodic monologue did not dismiss the dialogue in every country at the same time. New stylistic features such as the 'lazy' bass-line, the short expressive phrase so often ending in a sigh and silence, the enthusiasm for the concluding minuet and the undriven three-movement form rather than the older slow-fast-slow-fast type, were all symptoms of a new virus that had begun its infection at least a generation earlier. But the fever was yet to come. Bach's *Galanterien* were simply popular (mostly French) dances added to the keyboard suite – his contribution to the re-unification of the styles; but his long-spun melodic lines could never by any stretch of the imagination be called natural or simple. 'Turgid, confused and artificial' was the response they aroused in Scheibe in 1737, and it is true that in the *galant* sense Bach never wrote a tune – he produced a melodic extrapolation from a sequence of harmonies. It is therefore less confusing to reserve the idea of *galant* for those composers who, moved by the beauty of the melody, proceeded downwards from it to produce supporting harmony. In contrast the truly baroque amalgams of Couperin, for instance, reveal a manner of musical thinking which looked upwards from the bass.

G. B. Sammartini (called 'of Milan' to distinguish him from the London oboist and others) wrote sufficient SSB sonatas during the 1740s and 1750s for certain stylistic patterns to be apparent. Whereas his accompanied keyboard sonatas of the same period are democratic in their sharing of material between violin and keyboard, the trios are all dominated by the top part. They are in either three- or two-movement form, ending with a minuet, in nature if not in name, at any speed from *gratioso* to *presto*. This slackening of intensity from first movement to last was a feature of the rococo idiom, and was not fully reversed until the end of the century and the finale-orientated symphonies of Beethoven. The style of these and many contemporary trio sonatas is so closely related to that of the string symphony that Rousseau lumped the two together as 'trio sonatas which the Italians more commonly call *Sinfonie*'. 'Affetuoso', Sammartini's favourite indication for an *andante*, was to contrast with a bustling, almost operatic *allegro*. Only the more heavily embellished slow movements, unsuitable for orchestral performance, are distinctive in Sammartini's output (see Ex. 1c); in most cases his simpler style is his best.

Confusion between G. B. Sammartini and his brother Giuseppe ('il londinese') was compounded by eighteenth-century publishers in England who merely accredited 'San Martini', or even 'Martini' on their title-pages. The thread is tangled still more by the one set of trios, which are indubitably the work of Giuseppe (*XII Sonatas for Two German Flutes or Violins With a Thorough Bass*), which display his brother's preference for a single melodic line plus accompaniment, frequently (as in Ex. 44) indebted to Vivaldi's solo concerti. As London's leading oboist ('the greatest performer on the hautboy that the world has ever known' according to Burney), Giuseppe naturally inclined towards wind scoring; the *traversi* parts of these trios sympathetically stay within the range of the recorder, or 'English flute'.

Ex.44 G. Sammartini (Son. 6, Walsh, 1730)

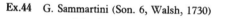

The same preoccupation with beauty of tone and niceties of articulation and embellishment that marks the instructions of Tartini also colours his sonata writing and evidently his performance: 'he doesn't play, he sings on the violin' was the contemporary report (see also p. 53). Most of his forty trio sonatas are in two movements only, with a balance of moods and speeds similar to that revealed by Scarlatti's single movement keyboard sonatas when arranged in the pairs the composer frequently intended.[1] Although his mellifluous chains of thirds and sixths may pall after prolonged exposure, they at least ensure reasonable participation for the second violin – perhaps, again, a teaching requirement. This lead was followed by Pugnani, one of the best trio writers of the following generations (though known to the present day purely by Kreisler's hoax[2]).

Literally dozens of Italianate composers of this age produced endless well-intentioned, fluently constructed and charmingly repetitive trios. The lack of motive force, of passion, of bizarreness or subjective feeling that one senses dispiritedly has gathered over this repertoire when viewed in bulk was dispelled by a literary wind from the north – the aesthetic of expressionism known as *Empfindsamkeit* (literally, ultrasensitivity). This was an aesthetic of extremes. There is no doubting the commitment and intensity of the best in this style, but the heights of expressionism can be embarrassing to a century that does not like to see men weep in public. Even the eye, following the tortured lines of this next example, its fractured phrase lengths and violent arpeggiation,

[1] See Kirkpatrick, *Domenico Scarlatti* (Princeton, 1953).
[2] Fritz Kreisler revealed his authorship of the infamous 'Praeludium and Allegro' in 1935.

is taken worlds away from the well-bred, ordered charm of Pugnani or Sammartini:

Ex.45 W. F. Bach

The *Empfindsamer Stil* is most easily connected with the two oldest sons of Bach, Wilhelm Friedemann and Carl Philipp Emanuel, but even there it was a minority cult. Neither Frederick the Great, nor the ubiquitous Burney on his travels approved of its mannerisms: 'long, difficult, fantastic and far-fetched' was

Burney's pronouncement on some of C.P.E.'s instrumental writing; and the King, unchanging in his preference for 'La France pour litérature, L'Italie pour la musique', encouraged the more anodyne productions of Graun, Fasch and his beloved flute teacher, Quantz. Although he is nowadays invaluable as a source for performance style (the *Versuch einer Anweisung die Flöte traversière zu spielen* (1752) deals with more general musical matters than flute playing), Quantz the composer succumbed too readily to the stereotype that his employer demanded. Kirnberger claimed at the time that the royal preference for triplet figuration, a real rococo mannerism, meant that all Quantz's sonatas were recognisable by their 'sugar-loaves':

By royal order, Quantz was prevented from publishing his music (as Zelenka had been in Dresden), and court performances must have been its only outlet. The small percentage of trio sonatas in his works was presumably restricted to performance by master and royal pupil, although violins and viola d'amore are included amongst some of his more interesting scorings. Remembering his approval of Telemann's essays in the 'learned style', it is not surprising to find many of his own works opening with a 'fugued' movement, wearing its contrapuntal learning lightly. 'M. Quantz,' said Burney,

after studying counterpoint, which he calls music for the *eyes*, went to work for the *ear*, and composed solos, duos, trios, and concertos; however, he confesses, that counterpoint had its use in writing pieces of many parts; although he was obliged to *unlearn* many things, in *practice*, which *theory* had taught him. . . .

Quantz's own instructions for composition, after suggesting that the quartet setting is the true touchstone of a composer (he was particularly impressed by examples from Telemann), continue:

A *trio* does not require quite so much laborious effort as a quartet, but if it is to be good, it does require almost the same degree of skill on the part of the composer. It has the advantage that the ideas introduced may be more *galant* and more agreeable than in a quartet, since it has one less concertante part.

The rules which follow emphasise that passage-work should be brilliant, that chains of thirds and sixths should not drag on *ad nauseam* and that 'it should be impossible to deduce which of the upper parts is the most important'. This last advice contradicts Italian practice, but was heeded by almost all the northern writers.

C. P. E. Bach was perfectly capable of producing the undisturbing trio settings that Quantz recommended. German interest in pedagogic music and the amateur market encouraged even the most wilful composers to produce 'leichte Stücke', easy pieces for teaching. But it is the infusion of *Sturm und Drang* into the bland texture of the *galant*, along with Bach's precise cultivation of the varied repetition of small units of melody, that raise his eleven trio sonatas above the norm. For the most part the scoring includes at least one flute, although one set is for two violins (Wot. 154–61), and a single sonata is scored for the unique combination of bass flute (recorder?), viola and continuo (Wot. 163). One imagines that only a clavichord, or possibly a very subdued *hammerklavier*, could serve for accompaniment. An extreme of *Affektenlehre* is the Trio in C minor, a particularly 'subjective' key for all classical writers, where a detailed programme represents the debate of the Melancholy and the Sanguine Man; the Sanguine Man wins. This curious, literary-inspired work was described as 'a truly impassioned tone dialogue' in the standard German musical dictionary of 1775,[1] which continued: 'Embryonic composers who hope to succeed with sonatas must take those of [C.P.E.] Bach and others like them as models'.

The 'fantasy-style', most suited to solo works, colours the slow movements of his concerted sonatas. That in E major (Wot. 162), with an optional scoring as trio for two flutes and continuo or single flute with obbligato keyboard, represents Bach at his best, unconstrained by royal or commercial pressures. It ends with the two flutes trailing off one after the other – a typical Berlin trick (Ex. 46).

The adjectives applied by Burney to C. P. E. Bach we would probably find more appropriate to his older brother Wilhelm Friedemann, who even today remains an outsider to the concert-hall. The best of his three trio sonatas (for two flutes in A minor) breaks off after a few bars of slow movement, sadly, but the patterns of trio sonata thought, unrestrained by limitations of instrument range, can be seen worked out in his keyboard sonatas in movements like the *Lamento* from Sonata No. 1, or the slow movement of No. 4 (Ex. 47 overleaf).

[1] By J. A. P. Schulz.

Ex.46   C. P. E. Bach

Ex.47   W. F. Bach

Wilhelm Friedemann may be responsible for the arrangement of a movement from one of his father's organ trios in the Triple Concerto (BWV 1044), but this is conjectural (Müthel is an alternative suspect).

One trend revealed by the output of the *empfindsam* school, to which can be added the names of Binder and Franz Benda for their trio sonatas, was the growing importance of the solo keyboard (particularly the expressive clavichord) over all other scorings for sonata writing. This was not a solely German phenomenon. Le Cerf had abused the practitioners of Italianate continuo playing many years earlier:

Formerly people of quality left to musicians by birth and profession the business of accompanying. Today they make of it a supreme honour. To play pieces in order to amuse oneself agreeably or to divert one's mistress or friend is beneath them. But to be nailed for three or four years to a harpsichord in order finally to achieve the glory of being a member of an ensemble, of being seated between two violins and a *Basse de Violon* at the opera, and to peck away, well or badly, a few chords which will not be heard by anybody – that is their noble ambition.

Whether his disenchantment arose from the presence of a second violin already filling in the harmonies or the growing simplicity of ensemble harmony in general is arguable. But the traditional title of an accompaniment for 'Violoncello or Harpsichord' could now be interpreted literally (Exx. 1c and 47, for instance, lose little by being played as string trios). Alternatively, the keyboard player could be elevated to the role of soloist, as in Avison's sonatas for the harpsichord, 'with Accompanyments for Two Violins and Violoncello' (1756–64), or the Viennese *divertimenti* of Werner. In England particularly, the trio sonata grouping had an extended lease of life as the normal accompaniment to the organ concerto after Handel.

Leopold Mozart, another vital teacher for the modern player, marks the decline of the keyboard continuo in his trios. In 1740 he published sonatas *da camera* and *da chiesa* for *due violini e basso* (where *basso* retained its baroque meaning of string plus keyboard continuo). After ventures into the *clavier trio* with *cembalo principalo, violino unisono ò violone cello* (*c.*1750), came the *divertimenti à due violini e violoncello* of 1760.

The strongest attraction on the European scene now came from the court of Karl Theodore at Mannheim, where 'the army of generals', as Burney admiringly termed the orchestra, draw almost all chamber forms after them and emanicipated the trio concept from its restrictive scoring. The final wall between the old world of restrained instrumentation and the new orchestrally-based one came tumbling down with titling that allowed performance 'either by 3, or with the whole orchestra' – Stamitz's Op. 1 trios when they appeared in Paris (*c.*1755). Their popularity was primarily as orchestral pieces, as their English title of 1763 revealed: 'Six Grand Orchestra-Trios proper for small or great concerts'.

The Mannheim style is probably the least keyboard-orientated style of the eighteenth century. But although the *need* for the keyboard may have declined, its presence continued almost to the end of the century, even when not specified. It is too easy to jump to the conclusion that when harmonic support was no longer necessary for coherence, the coloristic effect of the chordal instrument was also no longer required.

With the Mannheim school of primarily orchestral composers, a curious mannerism became apparent in their chamber works – what are best described as holes in the structure of pieces. The orchestral implications of this trio opening by Anton Filtz, for instance, are suggested by the gaps which strike the eye, and a continuo-less performance might be assumed, save for the fact that the bass part was specially figured for the second edition of 1768.

Ex.48   Filtz (Op. 3 no. 1)

The same proviso applies to the scoring of Stamitz' contemporaries and descendants; Richter and Toeschi for example, and even on to Haydn. Of more than seventy works listed by Hoboken for two violins and violoncello (called *Trios*, rather than *Divertimenti* in Haydn's *Entwurf-Katalog*), the vast majority require the colouring of a keyboard, at least for indoor performance. An accompanying keyboard is an alternative solution to the added double-bass line which is proposed for the trios (and the early Haydn quartets also) whose inner parts go beneath the bass line. Boccherini's experiments with a viola in place of the second violin (Op. 9) meant independence for the string group as a domestic ensemble free from keyboard, and suggest a final boundary to our *general map*.

If a terminal date for the trio sonata is required, then the last vestiges of true interplay between two violin lines occur in Mozart's Trio K 266, despite the efforts of modern editing to reduce the contribution of the second violin to a minimum.[1] At this point even the hardiest of trio sonata ensembles must call a halt; they have demonstrated their tenacity over all Europe for almost 200 years and more than 2000 works; the next century will offer them five *Bagatelles* by Dvořák.

Further Reading

BOYDEN, DAVID D., 1965, *The History of Violin Playing from its Origins to 1761.*

BURNEY, CHARLES, 1789, *A General History of Music.*

DART, THURSTON, 1960, *The Interpretation of Music* (4th edition).

DONINGTON, ROBERT, 1963, *The Interpretation of Early Music.*

HAWKINS, SIR JOHN, 1776, *A General History of the Science and Practice of Music,* 2 vols.

MACE, THOMAS, 1676, *Musick's Monument.*

MELLERS, WILFRID, 1950, *François Couperin and the French Classical Tradition.*

MOZART, LEOPOLD, 1756, *A Treatise on the Fundamental Principles of Violin Playing* (transl. Editha Knocker).

NEWMAN, WILLIAM S., 1972, *The Sonata in the Baroque Era* (3rd edition).

PINCHERLE, MARC, 1956, *Corelli His Life, His Work* (transl. Hubert E. M. Russell).

QUANTZ, J. J., 1752, *On Playing the Flute* (transl. Edward R. Reilly).

---

[1] The second violin's melodic contribution in bars 1–4 and 13–16 of the Trio is reallocated to the first violin in at least one modern edition.

ROWEN, RUTH HALLE, 1974, *Early Chamber Music*.

SCHENK, ERICH, 1955, *The Italian Trio Sonata* (Anthology of Music: Arno Volk Verlag).

SCHENK, ERICH, 1970, *The Trio Sonata Outside Italy* (Anthology of Music: Arno Volk Verlag).

SELFRIDGE-FIELD, ELEANOR, 1975, *Venetian Instrumental Music from Gabrieli to Vivaldi*.

WILSON, JOHN, 1959, *Roger North on Music*.

Index

Page numbers in italics refer to music examples